Books by David Wesley Soper
Published by The Westminster Press

The Spirit Is Willing
You Have Met Christ
Men Who Shape Belief
Highways to Faith
Major Voices in American Theology
These Found the Way

THE
SPIRIT
IS
WILLING

by

David Wesley Soper

THE WESTMINSTER PRESS / *Philadelphia*

© W. L. JENKINS MCMLVIII

Scripture quotations from the Revised Standard Version of the Bible are copyright, 1946 and 1952, by the Division of Christian Education of the National Council of Churches, and are used by permission.

Chapter 4, " The Man with the Gray-flannel Mind," was first published in *Christian Action* under the title " How *Not* to Become an Organization Man " and is used here with permission.

Library of Congress Catalog Card No. 58–9504

PRINTED IN THE UNITED STATES OF AMERICA

To
DAVID JONATHAN SOPER
son and colleague

CONTENTS

Point of Departure

PAUL TILLICH:
" Christ is the Spirit, and the Spirit is the Spirit of Christ. A Christian is one who participates in this new reality, that is, one who has the Spirit.

" I am convinced that much of the rebellion against Christianity is due to the overt or veiled claim of the Christian to possess God. . . . He is God for us just in so far as we do *not* possess him. . . . Only in idol worship can one believe in the possession of God.

" Do we still know that it is arrogant and erroneous for us to divide men by calling some ' sinners ' and others ' righteous '? "
> — *The Shaking of the Foundations,*
> pp. 132, 150–151, 154. Charles
> Scribner's Sons, 1948.

REINHOLD NIEBUHR:
" The doctrine of the Holy Spirit, as the third Person of the Trinity, is important, if we would understand that all forms of holiness and all signs of redemption in actual history are not merely extensions of human wisdom or human virtue but are the consequence of a radical break-through of the divine Spirit through human self-sufficiency."
> — *Faith and History,* p. 168. Charles
> Scribner's Sons, 1949.

" The possession of the self by something less than the ' Holy Spirit ' means that it is possible for the self to be partly fulfilled and partly destroyed by its submission to a power and spirit which is greater than the self in its empiric reality but not great enough to do justice to the self in its ultimate freedom. Such spirit can be most simply defined as demonic."

> — *Nature and Destiny of Man,* II,
> p. 110. Charles Scribner's Sons,
> 1951. Used by permission.

"Grace is synonymous with the gift of the ' Holy Spirit.' The Spirit is not merely, as in idealistic and mystical thought, the highest development of the human spirit. He is not identical with the most universal and transcendent levels of the human mind and consciousness. The Holy Spirit is the Spirit of God indwelling in man. But this indwelling Spirit never means a destruction of human selfhood."

> — *Ibid.,* pp. 98–99.

NELS F. S. FERRÉ:
"A fanatical devotion to doctrine . . . hides the face of God and rends the robes of humanity. . . .

"To let purity of doctrine become an end in itself is to choke the effectiveness of the spirit by means of the letter in order to honor the works of the spirit in the past. It is to kill the spirit by the works of the spirit! Dead doctrines cannot save the world."

> — *The Christian Faith,* pp. 87, 133.
> Harper & Brothers, 1942.

"The sign under which we conquer is forward to the fuller truth."

> — *The Christian Understanding of
> God,* p. 31. Harper & Brothers,
> 1951.

H. RICHARD NIEBUHR:
"Revelation, then, is either the fabulous clothing in which intelligible truth presents itself to people who have a low I.Q.; or it is the religious name for that process which is essentially the growth of reason in history.

"Christian life is cultural life [life in this world, life on earth] converted by the regeneration of man's spirit . . . the rebirth of the spirit of all men and the transformation of all cultural existence by the incarnate Word, the risen Lord, and the inspiring Paraclete.

"The present possibility of the transformation of temporal man into a child of God . . . [both socially and individually] is beyond the psychological mechanics of a shabby revivalism, with its mass production of renovated souls, . . . [it is also beyond] the sociological science of that part of the social gospel which expected to change prodigal mankind by improving the quality of the husks served in the pigsty. . . .

" The Christ who comes into the world comes into his own, and . . . it is Christ himself who exercises his Kingship over men, not a vicegerent — whether pope, Scriptures, Christian religion, church, or inner light — separate from the incarnate Word."

> — *Christ and Culture,* pp. 111, 205,
> 220. Harper & Brothers, 1951.
> Used by permission.

ALFRED NORTH WHITEHEAD:

" The worship of God is not a rule of safety — it is an adventure of the spirit.

" It is the business of the future to be dangerous. . . . In the immediate future there will be less security than in the immediate past, less stability. . . . But, on the whole, the great ages have been unstable ages — episodes in the manifestation of reason. . . . The moral of the tale is the power of reason, its decisive influence on the life of humanity. The great conquerors, from Alexander to Caesar, and from Caesar to Napoleon, influenced profoundly the lives of subsequent generations. But the total effect of this influence shrinks to insignificance, if compared to the entire transformation of human habits and human mentality produced by the long line of men of thought from Thales to the present day, men individually powerless, but ultimately the rulers of the world."

> — *Science and the Modern World,*
> pp. 192, 208. The Macmillan
> Company, 1925.

Foreword

Only one Spirit is " Holy " — the thrust of *Agapē*, the moral revolution that *now* makes men better neighbors in a better world neighborhood. The collective or " herd " mind of the past, and the individual or " rebel " mind of the present, not only can be, but are being, replaced, transcended, by the mind of the future, the community mind — by emotional and rational maturity, by self-hood and the will to preserve and cultivate selfhood in others.

Both laymen and clergymen have sometimes found one Christian idea nebulous, academic, essentially unavailable — the doctrine of the Holy Spirit (pneumatology).

This volume attempts to make one point as clear as possible — that you are not talking about the Holy Spirit at all unless you are speaking of the present-tense (always present-tense) *forward thrust* that moves, propels, drives individual men, religious and political groups, and mankind as a whole, *from within,* toward depth of freedom and breadth of brotherhood — *on earth!* It is not yesterday, or tomorrow, but *today* that the power to move and improve reaches us, re-creates our inner and outer life, and sets us growing — beyond all our standard varieties of lock-step *collectivism,* beyond the lonely anarchy of mere and sheer *individualism,* toward the full freedom and full fellowship called *community*. This explosive movement, this forward thrust, begins and continues in the mind, yet continually produces depth changes in religious and political structure.

You are talking about the Holy Spirit only when you are speaking of the holy thrust of Love which *now* intercepts and challenges all human mediocrity, in knowledge, in political and spiritual organization, and sets mankind *in motion* toward the unfinished image of God.

Beloit College   DAVID WESLEY SOPER

1

The Forward Thrust

"Not failure, but low aim, is crime." Aim at truth, God's truth for man, and you get life thrown in. Aim at life without truth, and you lose both truth and life. Hitch your wagon to a star. We have heard this good advice all our lives, but what in the world does it mean?

I read recently in a William Faulkner novel that to be a typical American is to love mediocrity. Personally, I share the hope that the statement is not true.

Our nation, generally speaking, assumes that it has accepted Christ. But to accept Christ is to accept his Spirit, the call of God to moral growth, specific growth toward the stature of Christ inwardly and the universal fellowship of Love outwardly — a fellowship designed to embrace within one holy family saints and sinners, rich and poor, all men everywhere. To accept the call of the Spirit is to reject the love of mediocrity. There is no stopping place for the Christian: Christ is more than our morality, more than our society, more than our economic and racial caste system, more than our religion. He is a plus sign beyond all present maturity. The call of his Spirit cannot be evaded. Man is so constructed that he can never really admire, or deeply respect, any lesser call.

This is the Christian's grandeur — and his misery. Christ is his grandeur. There is no higher standard than the perfect Love that accepts us as we are for what we may become — in his world, in his way, and in his strength. But Christ is also the Christian's misery: a wide gap inevitably remains between our noblest present achievement and God's kind of love — steady and steadily creative — made flesh in Jesus.

Moral growth toward the stature of Christ and the universal fellowship of Love — this is the demand of the Spirit upon every century, every society, and every individual soul — at every moment.

Alongside this demand, the call of *Agapē,* let us examine ourselves and our society. Our motion pictures, with many encouraging exceptions, seem designed for adults with twelve-year-old minds. Technically speaking, an adult with a twelve-year-old mind is a moron. We Americans spend endless hours in these movies. What we see long enough makes us over in its image. Our newsstands contain little news and they seldom stand: our magazines, with many important exceptions, are glittering appeals for mediocrity and conformity, for standardized boredom, for organized "ho-hum"; they illustrate spiritual cretinism — the body has grown large, the mind small.

Our public schools, with many welcome exceptions, appear to perpetuate and guarantee mediocrity in our taste, our American standard of loving; for we are what we love. Often enough, our schools seem little more than organized baby-sitting industries; their course offerings, generally speaking throughout America, are as bare as Mother Hubbard's cupboard — first of all in content, and even more in coverage. Undoubtedly, there are as many creative personalities among teachers as among preachers, yet the social life (especially the unofficial social life) that accompanies school life sometimes provides detailed training in depravity.

Our homes, with many noble exceptions, seem characterized by low aim; since low aim is crime, at birth we often give our children a low blow; from delinquent parents delinquent children grow — and there are many kinds of delinquency. Lack of interest in moral growth is often firmly formed and unchangeably hardened in our homes first, our schools second. Growth toward what? Nobody is better than we are! Christ himself is not higher than our way of life! Is not this, in some degree, in frightening degree, our American mental habit?

Saddest of all, our religion, though Christian in name, is often typically American in content. It frequently sanctifies, and petrifies, the *status quo*. Here a minister is on the move toward the practical growth of Love. There a layman feels deeply called toward the better that is not yet possessed by any man. Sometimes the minister has domesticated his idealism in realism, lowered his aim, and become an ambitious manipulator of church machinery, a mere denominational promoter — like the manager of a chain store. Whether the minister caught the disease of life-without-truth — of what is called worldly success — from the layman, or the layman from the minister, it is impossible to tell. In any case the epidemic may not be, but seems, widespread in church and state.

We are indeed sub-Christian. However, the fact that we are sub-Christian is not our sin, but that we are content to remain so.

The first gift of the Spirit is divine discontent — God's call to growth, the forward thrust of *Agapē*. Exactly this is the meaning of the Sermon on the Mount. On any other terms the Sermon on the Mount becomes the Sermon in the Mud — " a tale told by an idiot, full of sound and fury, signifying nothing." The Sermon on the Mount, which must become the Sermon in the Market, means undeniably that we are half-finished souls in a half-finished civilization: we are called inescapably, irresistibly, to labor together for the practical growth of Love — in every dimension of our earthly life.

The Beatitudes, at the beginning of the Sermon on the Mount, add up to one idea: *Blessed are they who recognize their lack* — the poor in spirit who mourn, the meek who hunger and thirst after righteousness. No growth is possible for men and women who feel that they are as good as anyone, if not a little better; who think that they know it all, at least, all that is important. Religious bigots, for example, can never grow: they know it all — doctrinally.

In a railroad dining car not long ago, I heard the most profoundly Christian statement that has come to my attention in recent years. An acquaintance and I were discussing the men whose books had helped us the most: Toynbee, Sorokin, Dostoevsky, Tillich, Richard Niebuhr, Robert Calhoun. An Army top sergeant, a typical GI, overheard our conversation. He walked over to our table and said: " Will you give me the names of five books, the five best books you know, the five books that will do me the most good? *I'm tired of being so damned dumb!"*

He will find that he will need more than five books, though I listed five. He will find that he will never reach anything like adequate knowledge on any subject, or adequate virtue in any conduct — religious or otherwise. But the priceless statement came from his heart. There is one GI who is not far from the Kingdom of Growth. Indeed, he is already within it. The Kingdom begins with that attitude, and *only* with that attitude! No human will ever reach the place where he does not need to join the GI in his glorious remark, and mean it, from the heart. The only blessed Ph.D.'s are they who realize that Ph.D. means " Phenomenally Dumb." This neither justifies nor glorifies our present mediocrity: it means simply that moral growth is God's specific demand upon us and within us — the *presence* and *thrust* of the Spirit. The only saints who are truly blessed are they who say daily with quiet despair: " I'm tired of having accomplished so little in the Kingdom of Growth — for my friends, my loved ones, and myself! " The Beatitudes are wholly misunderstood when they are applied by one class of people called saints to another class of people called sinners. The greatest saint is the man with the keenest hunger and thirst for the stature and love of Christ, the creative energy of the Spirit.

To be truly blessed is to be a blessing. We are called to be not " the saved " but " the saving " — channels of God's quickening grace, the Holy Spirit, in our homes and our communities. Blessed are the merciful in heart, the peace-builders, the second-milers, for they shall be called, and shall be, the sons of God. Saints who have stopped growing, who have stopped hungering and thirsting, who are seeking to be blessed, and have ceased to be a blessing, have lost their Savior and their savor and are henceforth good for nothing. Nothing that any man or any nation has yet achieved is good enough. God's will can be spelled with four letters: m-o-r-e! More of the law which is Love (constructive action in all human relations); more of the Love which is law, and less of the love of mediocrity.

Most of us have never committed murder with a gun or a knife, but all of us, I suppose, at one time or another, have committed murder (as Jesus suggested) with belittling words, murdering someone's reputation, someone's self-respect. A man's reputation is sometimes more important to him than his life. We have committed murder with murderous looks, murderous attitudes, murderously divisive religion, a murderous caste system that excludes Negroes and Jews and all foreigners from the universal fellowship of Love, a murderous hysteria of national self-righteousness. Before God, America as well as Russia is substandard. Who says America is a saint and Russia a sinner? Americans. Even Europeans are a little doubtful. To what are we trying to convert Russia — our national self-righteousness, our American mediocrity? Are we trying to make over Russia in our image — or ourselves, and all men, in the image of God? In Jesus' words, " First take the log out of your own eye, and then you will see clearly to take the speck out of your brother's eye." (Matt. 7:5, RSV.)

What is adultery? We have been taught the barest minimum of an idea. We think adultery is no more than a sex relation outside marriage. On Jesus' terms, adultery is much more than that: in essence, it is complacent mediocrity in the love of wife or husband — to be a tightwad, a miser (and not alone with money) toward another member of your family! Adultery is to be satisfied with the second best in any human relation — the practice of self-centeredness, self-defensiveness, self-pity. Adultery is simply *lack* of helping, healing Love — lack of *Agapē*.

Our speech often betrays our real values, our low aims. In conversation, we are sometimes not only sub-Christian, but subhuman. In any twenty-four hours we seldom say anything worth saying, possibly because in the same period we seldom think anything worth thinking. The really hopeless soul is the man or

woman who is content to say nothing worth saying, to think
nothing worth thinking, in any day or night. Content to be dumb
— and therefore not only dumb but damned. The really hopeful
soul is the man of any age or station who is weary with his own
moral mediocrity — in speech, in action, in ambition — and de-
cides, with God's help, to be *on the ball* and *on the move* toward
Christ's freedom and fellowship for all.

What then is the meaning of the Sermon on the Mount? It
means one thing. As Jesus put it: "Be ye therefore perfect, even as
your Father which is in heaven is perfect!" (Matt. 5:48, KJV.) To
fulfill this commandment may be impossible. How would we
know? How often have we tried? To avoid or evade this commandment is equally impossible. Do we not usually judge our
neighbors by a perfect standard? Only in rare moments of great
self-honesty do we judge ourselves by the same standard. The
only man within a thousand light years of being a creative Christian is the one who daily sets his eyes, and his soul, on the practical growth of love — in his words, his work, his home, his
church, and his community. He recognizes with despair that he
does not possess this goal; he recognizes with joy that this goal
possesses him — and will never let him go!

BOOK ONE

BEYOND "COLLECTIVE MAN"

As Albert Schweitzer has emphasized, a multitude of modern men have little or no confidence in their own ability to separate sense from nonsense, to distinguish relative truth from relative error. Therefore, they accept ready-made the "party line" answers, the "standard" solutions, prefabricated for them by current majority opinion — by alleged or assumed "infallible" authorities — in matters social, economic, and political no less than in matters religious. In Schweitzer's view, a deep disdain for individual thinking, for reflective self-determination, characterizes our age — and, we add, the man with the gray-flannel mouth.

Collective man is man externally controlled. Whatever inner life he can be said to have is externally created and induced — is not his own — whether he is Protestant, Catholic, or communist, whether an adult, an adolescent, or a child.

The forward thrust, the presence and power of the Holy Spirit, moves men today and every day beyond "the herd" and "the horde" toward the beginning and growth of individual thought, of self-determination — the development of the King in man, the reflective and active bearer of the image of God.

The achievement of selfhood is not the place to stop, but without it community cannot begin. Without it, community shrinks or miscarries into collectivism. As Paul Tillich has pointed out: only individuals are capable of fellowship; the rest have social interactions.

2

When Youth Is Wiser than Age

Collectivism is a disease of weary and "wise" adults. Children are not born collectivists: they are offspring of an explosive and creative Spirit; collectivism is superimposed by mentally arthritic maturity, determined to "make over" the young mind in its likeness.

George Bernard Shaw once said, "Youth is such a wonderful thing, it's a shame to waste it on young people." Young people have energy, and older people sometimes have wisdom, but many, many older people would be willing to trade all their wisdom for half youth's energy.

On second thought I am convinced, in one sense at least, that young people are wiser than their elders. This is heresy, of course, but, heresy or not, I think it is true. Young people, as Jesus pointed out, look forward, and older people, too often, look backward. To look backward is pride, complacence, death. To look backward is to stop growing and start spreading. To the extent that older people adopt the backward look, their so-called wisdom is folly. To look forward is faith, humility, the honest realization that one does not have all the answers, not even all the questions. To look forward is to keep growing. In this sense, youth is wiser than age. Clearly this is what Jesus meant when he said: "Except ye . . . become as little children, ye shall not enter into the kingdom of heaven" (Matt. 18:3, KJV). Older folk too often seem more than honorary members of the Kingdom of the Past; minds and hearts that are *young* with the forward thrust of the Spirit are even now active members of the Kingdom of the Future.

Look at it this way: here is where we are, and out there, so far away as to be almost invisible, is where we ought to be. God's perpetual demand upon us is to move forward toward his will for us — his will which is always beyond our finest knowledge, our noblest virtue, our happiest social system. Where we are is a long way from where we ought to be. Obviously, therefore, if we start looking backward, it is only because we think we have fully arrived at God's will for us, which is simply to tell ourselves a lie. Pride is another word for dishonesty. We have not arrived, whether we are old or young. Christ's purpose for us is still beyond us, beyond all of us, beyond clergymen and laymen, beyond bishops and college professors and outstanding men of science. Humility is simply honesty. To keep looking forward is to realize the truth that we have not arrived — either in science or in dogma, either in economics or in theology.

The truth is ahead of us, not behind us. It can be reached, or more fully approximated, only by moving forward — eyes everlastingly to the front, to God's future for mankind, the future that was made flesh in Jesus. If youth looks forward, and age looks backward, then youth is wisdom, and age is folly. Obviously therefore, the biggest problem of youth is to *stay* young, to keep looking forward, never to succumb to the false luxury of the backward look, never to accept the lie of self-approval.

Age knows, or ought to know, more than youth, though the point can be debated. But what age knows is considerably less than what age ought to know. For us all, there is still a long road ahead to a reasonable approximation of God's will in society and in soul. The wisest man is keenly aware of the long road ahead; he is therefore humble, that is, honest. The half wise often accept the lie that they have arrived; they are the proud who have stopped growing. They are therefore less wise than the young who are looking, and moving, forward.

To repeat: the main problem of the young is to *stay* young, to keep growing, to keep moving. So often today the young are no longer young; they have the energy of youth but the folly of age;

they think they have arrived; they are world-weary collectivists; they believe they have all the answers; they have lost the wisdom of youth, the "bounce" of the Spirit — to look forward, to move forward, and never to stop growing, never to let honesty give way to dishonesty, humility give way to pride.

I once knew a young man of twenty-three who had a first-class brain. He could look down on the slower wits, and that was his trouble; that gave him the false wisdom of age; that made him feel that he had arrived, when in fact he had hardly begun. Filled with pride, he stopped growing, and became world-weary. He had all the answers, but did not yet know the questions. He came from one of the finest homes in America. His parents provided the best books, the best music, and genuine affection. His father was a writer, a popular radio commentator, and a devout church-man. At the age of twenty-three this youth felt that there were no more worlds to conquer. He was bored with life. He was old, older than his elders, many of whom were still looking and moving forward with humility. This youth, with the finest advantages in the world, leaped from the eighteenth story of a skyscraper. He committed suicide because he had lost the wisdom of the Spirit — to look and move forward toward better knowledge, better virtue, a better economic arrangement, a better political world.

In simplest terms, this twenty-three-year-old youth had lost faith. Faith trusts the future, and accepts the strength the Spirit imparts to move forward. When man looks backward, and only backward, faith is dead, and with it hope.

To *stay* young is the real problem. To stay young you do not have to believe that you know nothing. Rather, you have to believe that what you know, compared with what there is to know, is little more than nothing. The Holy Spirit alone creates in us this rare kind of humility.

I knew a man who was young at sixty. He said to himself, "What I now know, compared with what there is to know, is little more than nothing." At that time he was a doctor of philosophy, but not impressed with himself. It's a wise man who can survive a Ph.D. At sixty, he took a sabbatical leave from his profession, and went off to graduate school. He received a master's degree at sixty-one, and his thesis was chosen by the Library of Congress for its originality and value — one of two so honored that year throughout the United States. A year or so later, the same man started the study of German. He had forgotten all the German he had learned, as everyone does. He started in, not too proud to be a beginner. Before he died he had read the entire New Testament in German. He had similarly forgotten all he knew about Greek, and at sixty-two or sixty-three started all over again to master the difficult subject. He had read the Greek New Testament before he died. Doctors said that his joy in study gave him ten extra years of life. To him, they were the best years — filled with the glow and glory of youth, the eternal springtime of the Spirit.

To know more than we now do is not the whole task. To be better persons than we now are is also our assignment. The only way it can be done is to realize, no matter how good we think we are today, that our goodness, compared with the goodness yet to be gained, is little more than nothing. Pious prigs, who believe that they are good, are the damned. Genuine saints realize that the good to be gained is a long way beyond them. A wise youth put it this way: " Count yourself again, Big Boy, you aren't so many." Humility is simply honesty, the realization that one's present goodness is alarmingly small.

Christians are indeed " the called "; they are called — to *grow*. And there are many kinds of growth. One is growth in knowledge. Another is growth in Love, in responsible goodness, in dynamic godliness. One kind of growth often neglected is growth in usefulness, to make a better contribution than we have yet made to the achievement of working brotherhood, the holy goal of the Spirit. Every day we pray, and forget that we have prayed: " Thy will be done, on earth as it is in heaven " (Matt. 6:10, RSV).

Albert Schweitzer understood that the Christian is called to *grow*. At thirty, he was still young. Today he is definitely a young man in his eighties. At thirty he was a doctor of philosophy, but survived the disease; he was also a promising theologian, and a world-renowned organist. If he had then decided that he had arrived, he would have become prematurely old. He would have succumbed to *rigor mortis,* to pride, to the false wisdom of collectivists. He said to himself: "I know next to nothing. I have accomplished nothing." He then set about the long, arduous task of becoming a medical doctor, and reached his objective. With his wife, a nurse, he sailed for Africa, a neglected area of human need. He has never yet felt that he has arrived. He has simply set himself the task of becoming more useful to his fellow men. He built a hospital on the edge of the forest primeval. The First World War destroyed it. After the war, he built a better one. He is still at work, reading, thinking, praying, walking in the Spirit, serving God's humanity, healing bodies, healing minds, healing souls. He is still growing, still young. He knows that God's will is far beyond our present achievements — in science, in religion, in statesmanship.

One night a few years ago a young man in his early twenties knelt down on a green lawn in the moonlight. He prayed with despair, with a broken heart: "O God, I have accomplished nothing for thee. Give me some good work to do for thee, for thy world, while life lasts." A few months later America began to hear from him. His name? Billy Graham. Whatever our view of his theology and his methods, this prayer seems genuinely Christian. The thrust of the Spirit moves us beyond the herd and the horde to individual selfhood, to personal creativity.

The religion of Jews and Christians may prove the final religion of this world for one simple reason: it accepts no human finality. It considers no institution and no idea of man exempt from the possibility, and the probability, of error. It sets us a goal, a goal as big as Christ's Spirit. This goal makes all our present achievements relative, fragmentary, preliminary. Even more, Christianity offers us the power to move, and keep moving, toward this goal; it puts this goal *inside* us — in the gift of the Holy Spirit.

Essential Christianity, the Spirit's presence and power, the poise and productivity of *Agapē,* is the most revolutionary force on

3

Resist Rigor Mortis *at Forty*

A perplexing question in our time is: "What to do with adults?"
Shooting them is probably illegal and may be immoral. If an adult
is something more than a man who has stopped growing at both
ends but not in the middle, he may be worth preserving. On the
other hand if an adult is more interested in where he has been
than in where he is going, his preservation may hardly be worth
the trouble.

It may be well to point out what is not so obvious as you think:
adults *are* people. Some, it is true, resemble pleasure, prestige, or
property more than personalities. An occasional adult resembles
the First National Bank — squat, square, and bulging with green-
backs. Another adult resembles a large tract of real estate — flat,
fertile, and high-priced. Still another adult resembles a parade,
with colors flying, bands playing, and a false alarm; he is going
nowhere noisily. Every fourth adult resembles the particular pleasure he pursues — a glass of beer, a country ham, a spring chicken.
What a man loves inevitably makes him over in its image — if he
loves it long enough. Adults naturally have loved their idols
longer than adolescents have, and have therefore become more
like those idols.

Some adults, at least, are people; they transcend their posses-
sions, are taller than their type. They are human. A human being
is involved in the natural world; he has a body and must consider
its needs. He is involved in society; he is part of everyone around
him, and everyone around him is part of him. More than this, he

is a spirit — a creation of the Spirit. He transcends every classification, cannot be satisfied with any possession, is capable of seeing his own faults and the shortcomings of his family, his bridge club, his church, his nation. He is one person, both finite and free, both flesh and spirit. In his flesh he is one with the beasts; in his spirit moves the Holy Spirit.

At rare intervals an adult is virtuous. His virtue lies in his awareness of his lack of it. When convinced of his virtue, he is no longer virtuous.

When an adult is most truly human, he is aware of certain spiritual facts. He is essentially a good creature whom God has made and loves, yet also in some degree a perpetual contradiction. He is a good being who sins in every thought, word, and deed. Further, his sins issue not from his flesh but from his spirit, his lack of faith, of courage — not from his finiteness, but from his refusal of freedom. The Spirit offers him individuality, personhood; he prefers collective anonymity, individual nonentity.

So far as we know, God looks at every adult and sees two things — the potential saint that is in him, and the actual sinner that he is. God suffers the sinner and labors to bring forth the saint. Since God is eternally interested in each adult, we must be also. In every adult walks a sinner who is the raw material of a saint. For the sake of the saint which every adult may become, the Spirit is willing, and we ought to be willing, to put up with the sinner every adult is.

The chief virtue of an adult is his maturity; his chief vice, the fact that his maturity is premature. An adult has already weathered the storms that sink many an adolescent's ship. He has gone over into the land of Nod and taken a wife from the daughters of men. When an adolescent, trembling on the precipice of matrimony, whispers ecstatically to his love, " I'm crazy about you," he is only speaking the literal truth. He is, precisely speaking, insane. Admittedly, it is a glorious kind of insanity, a good deal like dementia praecox, with alternating moods of grandeur and misery. An athletic coach once said to me, " From the time you're thirteen till you're twenty-three, you're practically insane anyhow." He justified high school and college athletics on the ground that they use up adolescent energy, usually attached to an unbalanced mind. Athletics, he said, help youth over fool's hill.

Whether or not adolescence and insanity are two words for the same thing, adolescence and immaturity are. By definition an adolescent is immature. His chief danger is that he may mistake his immaturity for maturity, and thus become a standard collectivist adult. At the ripe old age of eighteen he knows more than he ever knew before or will ever know again. The difference between high school seniors and college freshmen is the difference between pride and humility. A high school senior is a big shot, a college freshman a little nobody. Mark Twain said that when he was fourteen years of age he considered his father very ignorant, but when he was twenty-one he was amazed to see how much the old man had learned in seven years. Adults, at least, are safely past the epidemic called adolescence.

Not only have they solved the knotty problem called romance, but they have paddled their canoe safely through the rapids of finding a job. Our society presents every adolescent with a thousand and one careers. All he has to do is choose — among the whirling possibilities. I recall my father's vigorous disapproval when, as a high school sophomore, I concluded that I wanted the " security " of a job as railway postal clerk. The pistol the clerk carried appealed to me, and the idea of free travel, which would probably have turned out to be monotonous shuttling between country villages forty miles apart. An adult has gotten through the difficult business of selecting a career. Whether he has chosen wisely or not, no one knows, least of all himself. A recent college graduate was a Phi Beta Kappa in chemistry; immediately upon graduation he accepted a highly paid job stuffing sausages. He may eventually emerge from a sausage and find a career in chemistry, but for the moment he is a case of arrested development.

The glory of adult maturity is great. The sorrow of adult maturity is the fact that it is always premature. An adult is inevitably inclined to complacency, collectivism, and conservatism. He has finally secured " a couple of bucks," and is both proud of them

and anxious to hang on to them — though he developed stomach
ulcers, falling hair, and fallen arches acquiring them. The trouble
with being an adult is neither less nor more than intellectual,
moral, and spiritual *rigor mortis*. Yet the dead can be resurrected;
the quick can be redirected. Miracles of this kind are the daily
work of the Spirit.

The collectivist hardening of adult arteries (especially in
churches) has been described by Mildred Whitcomb: " The real
trouble is that God and the *status quo* are worshiped at adjacent
altars." She may have been overly generous. It would often be
true that God and the *status quo* are worshiped at the *same* altar;
the *status quo* itself is often worshiped as God. The miracle of
the Holy Spirit is the exclusion of the *status quo* from the Trinity.

The characteristic sin of adulthood is this: the partial and pro-
vincial become the absolute. We mistake our society for a Christian culture, are unaware that both Christianity and democracy
are likely to continue long after our embattled bureaucracy has
collapsed of its own weight. We do not see that Protestantism has
always sanctified *laissez-faire* economics, as Catholicism has always sanctified the feudal caste system or hierarchy. We mistake
our relative American values for ultimate Christian goals. The
typical American, once a rugged individualist, is now a despiritu-
alized collectivist, a standardized suburbanite, a psychological so-
cialist, a moral dwarf. When anything less than God is regarded
as absolute and final, an idolatry is created; every idolatry is destructive, for the demonic is good human energy in the service of
a false absolute. We adults continually provoke youth to rebellion by our premature pride. We church folk perpetually provoke
worldlings to secularism by our premature piety.

Official boards, like faculties, are notoriously timid. As a pastor,
my church officers often reminded me of the twelve spies who
went on a tour of reconnaissance into Canaan. Of the twelve who
ventured forth, ten returned to say the land could never be conquered. Two only, Joshua and Caleb, moved by the Spirit, returned to say that the job that couldn't be done could and must
be done at once. My official board usually presented the same

statistics — ten against, two for, every forward step. Faculties (students too) often vote the same way. People paralyzed with premature maturity always block the path of progress. Adults, reawakened by the Spirit, pray daily, " O Lord, forgive us our righteousness."

As Dorothy L. Sayers so well states it:

" All normal children . . . look forward to growing up. ' Except ye become as little children,' except you can wake on your fiftieth birthday with the same forward-looking excitement and interest in life that you enjoyed when you were five, ' ye cannot see the Kingdom of God.' One must not only die daily, but every day one must be born again."

Alexander the Great was not as great as he has been said to be, for he mistakenly thought that there were no more worlds to conquer. He was prematurely senile. Lot's wife was prematurely old; she looked back instead of looking ahead. The " pillars " of our churches, like Lot's wife, and for the same reason, are sometimes pillars of salt.

Possibilities for creative activity abound, but a possibility can only become an opportunity when an adult possesses, or newly acquires, a strong and steady *desire* to create — the productive thrust of the Spirit. Opportunities for creative activity can only be turned into creative actualities when the desire becomes a determination.

All hope of progress rests in the fact that a human being not only is involved in the society that has nurtured him, but also stands above it and is able to see its faults. The real hope of world constitutional government is the fact that each human soul transcends the parochial sovereignty that governs him, and can envision (and labor to realize) a political state as broad and inclusive as humanity. The real hope of a reunited Christendom is the individual's capacity to transcend his own denomination and think in world terms. An important creative opportunity in our time is the desperate need in every human collective (every labor union, every association of manufacturers, every consumers' co-operative) for individuals who can and will think in larger terms than group egoism. Groups are always more selfish than individuals; nations, said George Washington, can never be led beyond their own interest. Denominations likewise? The individual Christian not only can but must see farther than the selfishness of his race, his class, his clique, whether economic, political, or religious, and embody in his words and deeds the inclusive perspective of the Spirit. If adult Christians are not going to be the " holy remnant," the " creative minority," the critics of the group egoisms that turn our cosmos into chaos, God will raise up other agents of his grace!

One creative opportunity, always close to home, is the neglected art of forgiveness. The sin in the neighbor in some sense is also in the self. Forgiveness requires the ability to see the potential saint in the actual sinner; this ability is the presence and perspective of *Agapē*.

One's home and one's job, including the job of being a student, offer immediate opportunities for breakthrough beyond subspiritual collectivism. Creation is never a long way off; like the Kingdom of Heaven, it is always near at hand. Take an objective look at yourself; other people do; the Holy Spirit does. It is part of the glory of being human that (in some degree) a man can look at himself objectively. Spiritual growth always results when a man examines himself honestly in the love of God, contrasts himself with Christ, the saints and the martyrs, and sees with occasional clarity his own room for improvement.

Creative opportunities are everywhere. Every church is primarily a workshop. The true church is built, not on the pride that looks to the past, but on the humility that looks to the future. The true church is the explosive presence of the Spirit in the minds and deeds of men.

My mother long demonstrated that an adult can be something more than a cipher in the collectivist sea. In every community where we lived, while my father was pastor of the central church, my mother sought out the neglected folk on the edge of town or in the slum area across the tracks. She made it her business to start a Sunday school among them, with little or no help, and keep it going for no other reason than love. At seventy-three years of age she taught twenty-five hundred children every week in the public schools of St. Petersburg, Florida. She fired their emotions with hymns, the distilled fragrance of the worship of the centuries, and their imaginations with the heroic tales of the Bible, including its supreme story, of the Love of God made flesh at Bethlehem and Pentecost, the Love that was resisted by the premature religious maturity of Jerusalem and the premature political maturity of Rome. At seventy-four my mother taught fifteen hundred colored children every week. At seventy-eight, with father no longer at her side, and crippled with arthritis, she taught thirty children a week in her own living room. She taught twenty the day before she died. She opened young hearts to the future; she introduced young minds to the Spirit. She once explained to me: "I always see the future in the present. A child may be something of a nuisance today; I see in him a great and useful citizen, a channel of the Holy Spirit, tomorrow."

4

The Man with the Gray-flannel Mind

I have no way of knowing whether or not there are actual breathing individuals who hear, from birth to death, *no absolute call* — to depth and breadth, to height and permanence of life. I am reasonably certain, and would be prepared to argue, that no one has ever lived or now lives without feeling (sometime, somewhere, in some degree) *the forward thrust,* the Holy Spirit. According to the Fourth Gospel: the Light (which is God) is *within* every man. (John 1:4, 9.)

It is one thing, of course, to experience the thrust forward, the impulse to evolution, the Holy Spirit, *occasionally,* and quite another to experience it more or less *constantly* — to be moved, actually moved, by it beyond the collective unconscious, beyond adult infantilism, to the threshold of reason, the beginning of growth, the dawn of creation. After long struggle, however, I have given up the common idea that some men are capable of thinking, of growing, whereas others are not. I believe rather that some men have been born — intellectually, *inwardly* (a second birth indeed!) — while others (so to speak) are still in the womb. (John 3:7.)

Recently I was talking with an old and trusted friend — in part a religious collectivist. As a soldier, he spent a year in Europe. He has had wide experience — has seen much of life. His IQ is high; high also are his sense of humor and his sense of honor. At his suggestion, not mine, we began to discuss religion. Presently he said: "Fellows like me haven't time to separate wheat from straw

in matters of faith; we are farmers; we feed America. We have
to take our preacher's word for it."

Leadership is noble and necessary; it develops, however, only
when men think for themselves — and choose the louder voices
among them to express their thoughts; it is wholly different, different *in kind,* from the collectivist belief that a few men must
do our thinking for us. Whatever happened to the Hebrew and
Protestant idea — *the priesthood of every believer?* That idea (in
the sixteenth century) started a major revolution, economic as
well as ecclesiastical, yet was simple enough: God (and the world
of truth) are available *directly* to *every* thinking mind. The individual (if he will put forth the effort) not only may, but can, examine and judge for himself — in *the Bible* not less than in life.

Protestantism exists in name only when its central idea (every
man's ability and responsibility) has withered on the vine. When
Protestantism is alive and alert, minorities (whether of many or
of one) are protected and respected in their right to disagree with
majorities. When Protestantism is dead, democracy, as a working
political system, is dead also, for its central idea, too, is the dignity,
the responsibility, of every man. Free governments stand or fall
with the individual's capacity (developed or undeveloped) to separate sense from nonsense in the applied religion, the applied ethics, called " politics."

The democratic way of life is not majority rule or ruin, but the
firm protection of minorities in their right to be different (without penalty): for example, the right of Catholics to be Catholics
in a Protestant society, and vice versa; the right of Jews to be Jews
in a gentile society, and vice versa; the right of Negroes to be
Negroes (without discrimination) in a white society, and vice
versa.

The gray-flannel mind is externally directed and controlled; it is
subpersonal, subconscious, subhuman. It is common not only in
Baghdad-on-the-Subway (Manhattan), but also on Lake Michi-
gan, in Monaco, Morocco, and Mombassa. It is neither awake nor
asleep, but somewhere between. The gray-flannel man does many
things with his eyes open, goes through many motions, from

dawn to dusk, but neither knows why nor cares that he is entitled
to ask.

Sigmund Freud introduced the idea that perverted sexual behavior is infantile sexual behavior — undeveloped, undifferenti-
ated — prolonged into adult years. Exactly in the same way, the
collective or herd mind is the infantile mind — in the brain vault
of an adult; it is not child*like* but child*ish*. There is no infantilism
in infants! You have met it in the man in your mirror! It is
strictly a B.C. disease — Beyond Childhood. Some infantilism is in
us all, and we must learn to detect it, to be on our guard against
it. It delays not only the forward movement of mankind as a
whole (after all, the evolution of the human race seems a distant concern); of greater immediate importance, to us and finally to all, adult infantilism impedes our own participation in
life.

According to Gerhard Groote, "Vanity it is, to wish to live
long, and to be careless to live well." Young people are rightly an-
noyed when older people say to them, "When you have lived as
long as I have, you will see things as I do." It is just this a youth
fears most! The one thing he would like to avoid — if he only
knew how — is the hardening of the mental arteries he sometimes senses in adults. The fact that one has lived a long time
proves only that he inherited good physical equipment; it says
nothing (automatically) about greater wisdom. Methuselah, who
died at the ripe old age of 969, enjoyed length, if neither height
nor depth, of life; Jesus died at thirty-three! The oldsters (the
Pharisees) told him that he was crazy, or that his wisdom would
ripen with the years. Perhaps their wisdom was not only ripe but
overripe; it is only one step from ripe to rotten.

Majority opinion is not always a good guide — on any subject.
Majorities have supported every wrong cause in history (for example: slavery, anti-Semitism, and segregation); majority support
made the wrong cause the strong cause. Mobs are majorities too.
It is only fair, of course, to point out that the masses are often
falsely identified with so-called majority opinion. History sometimes hears only the loud voices of dictators, the leather-lunged

orators who claim to speak for the people. If the truth were known, the masses have probably seldom believed what they were said (or told) to believe; their rulers simply controlled the noise-making machinery of pomp and propaganda. All we know is what the rulers said; the people were not permitted to speak (itself an evidence that they could not be trusted to speak the party line).

Majorities, as we know them, are blocks of opinion; it is sometimes difficult to distinguish between blocks of opinion and opinionated blockheads. In so far as majorities represent unexamined prejudices, they are evidence of adult infantilism — in epidemic proportions. Official majorities helped crucify Christ — and Woodrow Wilson's League of Nations. Southern majorities were not overly critical of Lincoln's assassin, John Wilkes Booth. The Hindu majority finally outvoted Buddhism, and packed it off, bowl and yellow robe, to China, Tibet, and Japan. The Jewish majority resisted Jesus, the Second Moses, for the same reason they resisted the First. They found Moses hard to swallow, and his commandments hard to follow; again and again they returned, or desired to return, to the calf of gold and the Egyptian fleshpots. The majority of Southern Europeans did not think with Luther in the sixteenth century — nor have they thought with him since.

Undoubtedly, majorities are as capable of creative vision as their component individuals; but capacity for vision and the flame and thrust of its presence (the Holy Spirit) are not the same thing.

The adult infantile is well known in our society. His name is legion. You have met him times without number in politics — "the man with the gray-flannel vote." In our system of government, we choose between parties, even more than between persons. In an election, as in a wedding, we marry the whole family; when we cast our ballot for a political leader, we adopt all his relatives. These relatives, as well as the leader, ought to be looked over in advance! You expect a few horse thieves in any family album — but enough is too many! And the family may be tainted with insanity! The candidate himself may bathe occasionally; it is his poor, and even more his rich, relations who may prove a collective embarrassment.

The political adult infantile (whether plutocrat, technocrat, or independent) simply goes along for the ride; thinking about issues is not his strong point; the desire for information is not his burning passion. When he hears the call of God to constructive action, he replies: " Here am I, Lord. Send George! " He is essentially a somnambulist — voting in his sleep. If he considers the Democratic Party radical, progressive, equalitarian, he never asks what the words mean; he merely votes pro or con — usually for Bible, home, and Mother with proper Republicans everywhere. Conversely, if he considers Republicanism another word for reaction, retrogression, and *rigor mortis,* he starts making a noise like a Democrat; again he goes along for the ride — neither awake nor asleep. He adopts the " pose " of the passionate liberal, the consecrated nonconformist — as unthinkingly as he formerly adopted the " repose " of the G.O.P. Unlike the elephant, he has a short memory — and unlike the jackass, he has more kick than pull. Whatever his political affiliation, he wears blinders on his eyes, and a flannel blanket on his mind. Potentially (and actually) he is a child of God, with the intelligence to grasp (deeply and creatively) the words of God; it is by his own choice, his own lethargy, that he becomes in practice a parasite, a bench warmer, a nonparticipant, a nonentity.

In point of fact, the adult infantile is only a little more common in politics than in religion. In every congregation sits the man with a gray-flannel faith. He says to himself or aloud: " The King James Version was good enough for Paul; it is good enough for me. . . . I never read the Bible, but I always have one in the house — it's insurance against warts. I usually check my brain at the church door, along with my rubbers and umbrella. Thinking about life and its meaning makes people unhappy. I go to church to worship. . . . I neither buy nor read modern books about religion; as a child, I got it all straight in Sunday school. I don't want to be confused."

I may be wrong, but I believe I have found more infantile

adults, more unthinking men, outside than inside the churches. The vacant mind is not uncommon among folk allergic to religion — whose faith is a vacant lot. Party-line members of the cult of indifference say to themselves or aloud, " I was forced to attend Sunday school as a child — and I want no more of it." The man with the gray-flannel no-faith tries to keep up to date in his profession; it is only in his religion that he is a somnambulist, in a state of arrested development, still operating for or against the unexamined information he received as an infant, and has kept as an infantile adult. A mind can be as firmly closed *against* as *for* its childhood religious instruction. In either case, a closed mind, like a closed room, is filled with stale air. Gray-flannel mental suffocation characterizes the negative as well as the affirmative pose. Not to attend church, merely from force of habit, is a gray-flannel farce. There is only one good reason for attending church: to think straight — that is, to pray aright.

The adult infantile (whether churched or unchurched) says, in effect: " My religion, may it always be right; but right or wrong, wise or foolish, ideal or idiotic, my religion — especially if my religion is no religion."

The same man is quick to condemn communists for shifting their minds into neutral as their first act of party loyalty; he is quick to condemn Catholics for gray-flannel faithfulness to meatless Fridays. It is only his own " received faith " he has not the intestinal fortitude to examine. Naturally, he does not want to start an argument — nor is he capable, with his present information, of starting one worth starting. Luther (Protestants believe) started an argument worth starting, and kept it going — the right and duty of the individual to examine and judge for himself the meaning of Holy Writ and papal decree. Piffle people no doubt start piffle arguments — to prove incontestably that they are piffle people. They thus demonstrate their " uniquity " in public. Jesus, on Christian terms, started an argument worth starting — an argument with unthinking Hebrew conformity, the gray-flannel faith of the Pharisee. Both Jesus and Luther found something radically insufficient in their own " received faith "; they started no arguments with strange creeds or unfamiliar dogmas; they challenged the known, the established, the accepted — especially when these were followed without comprehension.

The presence of the Holy Spirit (in others or in us) starts an argument worth starting — with our own adult infantilism, our own fear that an examined political creed will collapse, an examined faith will fail. When the Holy Spirit comes, said Jesus (in effect), " He will convince the world of the sin of somnambulism, self-righteousness, and surface judgment" (John 16:8, RSV, paraphrase). He will bring not " peace, but a sword " (Matt. 10:34, RSV).

Arthur Koestler, Ignazio Silone, and Richard Wright became communists out of passionate disgust with existing economic, political, and religious inadequacy; they left the Communist Party when they discovered they could no longer think for themselves — that they were required to accept without question the Central Committee's gray-flannel infallibility. A friend of mine became a Roman Catholic out of sheer disgust with Protestant doctrinal and denominational diversity; he left Catholicism when he discovered that he was free to think only " with the church," that Roman clarity (in his view) was cloudy with error, that error itself was exempt from examination — a hand-me-down from gray-flannel hierarchies.

There are many kinds of tyranny; the worst is not imposed by the sword upon adult bodies, but by fear — even by the threat of hell — on the sensitive imaginations of children. It sometimes happens in Protestant as well as Roman Catholic churches — and in capitalist as well as communist countries.

Many a man has joined a Protestant church to escape the secular vacuum; not a few have returned from Protestantism to secularism when they have learned that their particular denomination required them to agree, or get out — on highly debatable dogmas. Intellectual agreement is sometimes the end of a discussion; it ought never to be the required beginning. The height of egoism is reached when we are willing to have full fellowship only with those who agree with us.

Gray-flannel minds often abound in the world of business. They have found thinking difficult, especially thinking about religion — direct wrestling with life and its meaning; they have become intellectual (that is, moral) dwarfs, *by choice*. With stuffed pockets but stunted souls, they have gone forth selling bonds — to the sound of trumpets.

Gray-flannel fraternities and sororities, with their infantile conformities, are familiar on college campuses. There are many exceptions — there is nothing automatic about it — but not infrequently the fraternity type (who wears the right clothes, drives the right convertible, and "sobers up on wood alcohol") has given up thinking — not only for Lent but for always. He wears a mute on his conscience, a silencer on his mind. No divine call reaches him; he stifles the whisper of the Spirit. Presently he will leave the halls of ivy, graduated but not educated — a polished nincompoop, a man of the world, half alcoholic and all vacuum, the cause of nothing, the effect of everything.

Not often, but sometimes, and always elsewhere, colleges are operated by gray-flannel faculties and adult infantile administrators. Independence of thought — just plain thought about anything — is rare; administrative and faculty fuzz-brains sometimes prefer to struggle along without it. Thinking is not too common, to be sure, yet shepherds can never really bank on the unthinking loyalty of their sheep — in politics, in religion, or in education.

The gray-flannel labor leader was a recent comedian on television; his followers, apparently, asked him no questions; he told them no lies. The capitalist was once the dreaded foe of the toiler; if only occasionally, it is now the labor boss who picks the workers' pockets and absconds with their funds.

A husband and a wife sometimes share a gray-flannel marriage; one has become a tyrant, the other has surrendered the right to an opinion. An occasional bachelor too is an adult infantile, fearful of the high cost of monogamy — the gray-flannel fainthearted who never won fair lady.

The Spirit of God wrestles with us, individually, inwardly, constantly, creatively; it is he who resists our unthinking capitu-

5

Communist " Brotherhood Without Freedom "

The *status quo* and the call of God are never quite identical. No present system of government, no present economic arrangement, no present form of religion, in Russia, in Rome, or in America, is either sufficient or self-sufficient. The full realization of reason, the will of God, in man and society is not yet here. We are thrust by the Holy Spirit toward a better future; that future will contain personal freedom and social fellowship, on a world scale, not only beyond our present practice, but also beyond our present imagination. " Eye hath not seen, nor ear heard, neither hath it entered into the heart of man, the things which God hath prepared — and will achieve on earth, in and for mankind, the object of his love." (I Cor. 2:9, KJV, paraphrase.)

So strong in us all is the thrust-toward-community, the Holy Spirit, that it sometimes produces, in our limited minds, distortion as well as creation. The " collective distortion " of the twentieth century (from our point of view) is called communism. In its haste to achieve economic brotherhood, it sacrifices personal freedom. Since personal freedom, as well as economic brotherhood, is the demand of the Holy Spirit, communism finds itself, on this point, at war with the Spirit.

Similarly, capitalism (the " individual distortion ") has something to contribute, but cannot be fully (or automatically) identified with the growth of community. In Holland, I asked the European Christian Karl Barth why he did not visit America. He replied, " I see very little to choose between freedom without brotherhood in America, and brotherhood without freedom in Russia."

Freedom without brotherhood is something other than freedom; it is anarchy; it is solipsism — the view that every man is an island; and it is loneliness. Brotherhood without freedom is something less than brotherhood; it is slavery. Men under common discipline form a fraternal order, but you are free to leave. A fraternity you cannot leave is a prison. At Sing Sing Penitentiary (incidentally, there were not many penitents) I once addressed a "brotherhood without freedom" of five hundred Protestants. In a nearby sanctuary, within the prison, a brotherhood without freedom of twenty-four hundred Catholics was at worship. Even in prison, you have freedom of religion! In communist Czechoslovakia I delivered a series of lectures to a "brotherhood without freedom" of five hundred Congregationalists.

What then, if any, are the communist values which the sacrifice of personal freedom has shrunk into vices? If we are to reject the "collective distortion" abroad and at home, we must try to understand it — to know, as clearly as we can, what we are rejecting, and why.

To begin with, communism is more than the nebulous fear that keeps wealthy middle-aged Americans awake at night; it is more than a convenient bogey, a handy target for Senators with little mental substance; it is more than a scapegoat for capitalist sins. It must have or be something in its own right, for the fear of it is the strength of America's un-American lust for conformity.

In our haste to slay the communist dragon, if we sacrifice personal freedom, are we not surrendering one of the chief things that distinguish our way of life from communism, and thus becoming lock step collectivists on our own account? If we sacrifice personal freedom, shall we not find *ourselves* at war with the Spirit? In Alan Barth's words:

"The American society — if it remains free — possesses a greater capacity for growth, a greater resourcefulness in meeting new problems and changing situations, than any closed society. In the long run, the free have triumphed over the enslaved."

Our traditional tolerance of wide diversity is now being under-
mined in ways dangerous to national security. Fear, and loss of
faith in freedom, have produced in us a paralyzing panic — you
might call it "the Sputnik panic."

However, it is never wise to underestimate a competitor.

As I see it, the communist bid for the imaginations of men con-
tains three positive ideas. Arnold Toynbee has pointed out that at
least two of these ideas (ecumenicity or "world-mindedness," and
humanitarianism or "the will to feed the poor") were borrowed
or plagiarized from historic Christianity, though the source has
never been acknowledged. Christians therefore cannot deny the
positive worth of these ideas without denying Christianity itself!

First: *the improvement of life on earth is man's serious business.*
That is, a bird in hand is worth two in the bush; the here is more
important than the hereafter; seventy good years before death are
more to the point than seventy-times-seven after death; *quality* of
life now has A-1 priority over life extended forever in *quantity.*
One half of Christianity, too, emphasizes that life on earth is
man's real concern, that the foundations of the future are laid in
the present; for this reason Jesus taught us to pray: "Thy will be
done, *on earth.*" The other half of Christianity, to be sure, is sometimes homesick for a heaven outside of time and history; it usually teaches, nonetheless, that present decision and direction determine man's destiny in the Great Beyond — that good works
proceeding *now* from good faith form the initiation fee, the fee of
acceptance into the Fraternity of the Pearly Gates.

Second: *the economic salvation of all men is to be sought actively, and finally secured.* That is, all men everywhere are included in the potential benefits of the Marxist atonement; to all,
the message (the Word and the Deed) must be taken, at any
cost in blood, sweat, and tears, by communist heroes, martyrs, and
missionaries. Christianity too possesses marked evangelical zeal.
"Go ye into all the world, and preach the gospel." Jesus said it
first; and, each for his own gospel, many men have said it since.
Paul, Mohammed, Francis of Assisi, Ignatius Loyola, John Wesley, David Livingstone, Marx, Lenin, Trotsky, and Albert
Schweitzer have preached, and practiced, a similar principle. At

his home in Paris, the French Catholic philosopher Étienne Gilson said to me with emphasis, "When Christianity ceases to be evangelistic, it ceases to be Christian." This means simply: if you have something worth selling, sell it; further, if you have something worth selling to one, it is worth selling to all — for all men are brothers in need.

Third: *the underprivileged toilers of the world deserve, and one day will gain, the power to rule.* That is, the world's wealthy have enjoyed long enough a free ride on the backs of the world's workers; in terms of the G.O.P., it is time to " get off and pull." Nothing except scraps and crumbs from the tables of the children of capitalism will be given the laborers of the earth that they themselves do not take — *by force,* if necessary. Every dog has his day, and the dogged masses are entitled to their day of power. Further, on communist terms, the masses, once in power, will bring all tyranny to an end; every man shall sit under his own vine and fig tree, and none (except the secret police) shall make him afraid. All distinctions of class and race and religion shall be abolished, and men will be brothers at last.

Christianity, too, teaches that the first shall be last, and the last first, that the kingdoms of this world, long held by the goats, will one day return to the sheep, that not the weak but the meek shall inherit the earth and delight themselves in the abundance of peace — for the Lord knoweth the way of the worker, but the way of the exploiter and the parasite shall perish. " Blessed be ye poor. . . . Woe unto you that are rich! " said Jesus — according to Luke (ch. 6:20, 24, KJV). Jesus' brother, James, thundered: " Go to now, ye rich men, weep and howl " (ch. 5:1, KJV). Both Isaiah and John the Baptist predicted the great leveling, when " every valley shall be filled, and every mountain . . . brought low " (Luke 3:5; Isa. 40:4, KJV). How could they have foreseen so clearly the Federal Income Tax — which does in effect, if only in part, create a classless society in the U.S.A.? Mary, the mother of Jesus, sang, the Lord " hath put down the mightly from their seats, and exalted them of low degree " (Luke 1:52, KJV). *Violent* overthrow of existing injustice, threatened unmistakably and on principle in the American Declaration of Independence, is threatened also in the words of Jesus and John: " The ax is laid to the root of the trees; every tree therefore that does not bear good fruit is cut down and thrown into the fire " (Matt. 3:10; 7:19, RSV).

Think for a moment of the strength of these ideas: direct relevance to the improvement of life on earth, missionary zeal for the salvation of all men, and hope for the earth's enslaved and exploited. The statement is not quite true, but is nonetheless challenging: " Communism is Christianity — in practical form." It is not enough to say, " But communists preach one thing and practice another." Who doesn't? Christians, too, bat less than .500. James accused the first-century Christians he knew of being stronger in words than in deeds; he wrote, " If a brother or sister be naked, and destitute of daily food, and one of you say unto them, Depart in peace, be ye warmed and filled; notwithstanding ye give them not those things which are needful to the body; what doth it profit? " (James 2:15-16, KJV). " Wherefore," said Jesus, " by their fruits ye shall know them." (Matt. 7:20, KJV.)

Combined with personal freedom, the communist ideas have much to contribute to the growth of community — both in depth and in breadth. To Christians everywhere, these ideas or values sound more than vaguely familiar. There is, of course, an accompanying vice which makes these values, in communist form, unacceptable. Nonetheless, their appeal (even in communist form) is all but irresistible to the hungry masses of Asia and Africa, and to Europeans as well — forced again and again to fight and die for France against Germany, or for Germany against France, then forced to live in the ruins, and all (often enough) in the name of Christ!

In other words, the free world must put up or shut up; we can and must do better than the communists — both in theory and in practice; if we do not make the world a better offer than theirs, ours will be politely but firmly rejected. To paraphrase Jesus' words, " Except your righteousness shall exceed the righteousness of the communist scribes and pharisees, ye shall in no case enter, or help build, heaven on earth." (Matt. 5:20, KJV.)

Unfortunately, the communist values are countered, crippled,

and accursed, by the communist fury of fanaticism — its deliberate and determined practice of tyranny, its total submergence
of the individual, issuing automatically and inevitably from its
claim or assumption of infallibility.

It all depends on how you answer one question: " Is the individual a means or an end? " It is true that great men serve men
greatly; on Jesus' terms, great men make themselves the servants
of all — they make themselves means to the end of common good.
Clearly each generation, both biologically and intellectually, is a
means to the enrichment or impoverishment of the next. We do
not, and cannot, live for ourselves alone. As Paul put it, " What
hast thou that thou didst not receive? " (I Cor. 4:7, KJV.) Jesus
said, " To whom much is given, of him will much be required."
(Luke 12: 48, RSV.) We owe our neighbor (far away and near
at hand, of every creed and clan) the same respect and helpful-
ness we ourselves demand. " Bear ye one another's burdens " (Gal.
6:2, KJV), said Paul; he also said, " Every man shall bear his own
burden " (Gal. 6:5, KJV). At times we must help our neighbor
carry his weight; all the time, if we can, we must strive to carry
our own.

We are, and of right ought to be, means to our neighbor's good
(I Cor. 10:24, RSV) — on Christian and communist terms, means
to our neighbor's salvation, lest his blood be required at our hands.
However, though we are, and ought to be, of use to other men,
contributors rather than robbers, lifters rather than leaners, blessings rather than burdens, it is also true that each of us is an end
in himself, not a means, a person not a thing, a subject not an object, a God-bearer and a child of God. The universe is as close to
us as it is to the top brass and the higher-income brackets. " All
things are yours " (I Cor. 3:21, RSV), said Paul. All things (other
than persons) are therefore means — whether churches or governments or economic systems. One and all, they stand or fall by
whether they help or hinder our joy in life — by whether or not
they remember that they are not our masters by the sword, but
our servants in the Spirit.

Since each man is (and ought to be) an end, in himself, to his government and his God, he is entitled to think, to speak, and to act on his own, with something more than formal freedom, empty of content. Freedom, when it is more than a word, means our right to disagree, where honesty demands it, and without loss of full fellowship, with the whims (and master objectives) of ruling men and majorities. We are entitled *not* to be smothered by the paternalism of secret police, by human bloodhounds; we are entitled *not* to have to look over our shoulders with fear, to whisper lest we be overheard; I saw that happen again and again in communist Czechoslovakia. Each of us is entitled as man, as *anthrōpos* (which means " the uplooker "), to look up, to stand up, to speak up. No progress of any kind has ever occurred except where individuals, like ourselves, did look up, stand up, and speak up; they called a spade a spade; they criticized and corrected injustice. When the individual is mentally choked into silence, into acquiescence and conformity, the collective distortion has conquered, in Russia, in Rome, or in America, and forward movement, the holy thrust of the Spirit, is dead.

The deadening vice of communism, then, is the fanatical assassination and burial of personal freedom, our human birthright; tall children of God become communist dwarfs — in mind, in moral vision. The name of this vice is tyranny; its fruit is slavery; its root is the assumption of infallibility. The view that any present understanding of man and the universe is exempt from the possibility of error is ludicrous. Who but a frenzied fanatic could take seriously the dogma that the party member is not to reason why — his duty is to do and die?

True, an army gets nowhere if every GI has equal authority with the commander in chief. On this basis, an army would march forth in as many directions as there are GIs. In peacetime, at least, precisely this is a good thing! Standing armies tend to stand first on freedom. GIs, each at his own home, on his own job, are the salt of the earth; all together in one place, they're a public menace. An army is not an unmixed blessing — though we can hardly do without one in wartime. No one should be forced to jump through hoops at the command of a top sergeant (other than his wife) in time of peace. In an emergency, an army may be a necessary evil, though always less necessary than evil. Men who sing as they march into battle stir the blood — especially when they march not to enslave the free but to free the slave. Under any conditions, however, the goose step may be fine for a goose, and for a man with the brain of a goose; it is not good enough for a man in the image of God, a man with the brain of a man.

The assumption of infallibility (by any man or group) is a joke, but it is not funny; it is tragic. Errors can never be acknowledged; error itself is exempt from critical examination. Men who point out errors receive permanent appointments in Siberia (when they are permitted to live!). Moral pygmies in uniform can make trouble in the world, but the dictator, sooner or later, forgets to push the right buttons on his robots. Political puppets or jumping jacks jump only when a dictator pulls the string; free men are self-starters; they are also self-propelled; soon or late, they always " pull the string " on the dictator.

" The improvement of life on earth " is a sane and glorious objective; we are not more than half evolved; but life is not improved when minds are bound and gagged. The " improvement of life on earth " as a settled goal, plus sacred personal freedom, in America we call " democracy." " The economic salvation of all men is to be sought actively, and finally secured." This good idea, plus personal freedom (of speech, of thought, of conscience, and of faith), is what Christians call the " growth of community." Turn about *is* fair play; " the right of workers to a vital share in the responsibilities of government," where personal freedom exists, is already, though inadequately, the American way. Without personal freedom (especially the freedom of the mind, freedom of thought and speech) the communist house of cards, tomorrow or the day after, comes tumbling down; Pharaoh's collective distortion crumbled before Moses and the Children of Israel. Collective distortion always yields (as time progresses) to the recovery of selfhood and the creation of community.

Book Two

BEYOND "INDIVIDUAL MAN"

The thrust toward selfhood is sometimes called "original sin." Majorities tend to fear it as subversive nonconformity. As Nels F. S. Ferré has suggested, original sin, understood as the struggle for self-determination, is an original necessity. Unless a person develops selfhood he has no self to contribute to the common good, the common growth. However, to stop at the achievement of selfhood is to frustrate the growth of fellowship.

When selfhood, in a measure, is achieved, an individual (whether adult or adolescent) may do one of three things: he may retreat to collectivism, to external authority, driven by loneliness; he may remain a mere individual, in the arrested development called solipsism (isolated selfhood) — thereby creating the social miscarriage named anarchy; he may also move forward toward the self-transcendence called community — thereby achieving the foundation of continued selfhood, enriched by freedom, exalted by faithfulness, fulfilled in depth and breadth of fellowship.

Precisely this third choice, the move beyond "individual man" to "community man," is (today and every day) the forward thrust of the Spirit, the presence and power of God.

6

" No Man Is an Island "

From one standpoint, there are only two main classes of people: idealists who say, " There ain't no hell! " and realists who say, " The hell there ain't! " One kind of hell, an inferno of agony, is the lock step or goose step of collectivism, the perpetual nightmare of existence under the surveillance of secret police, the incurable claustrophobia of life without freedom. The other kind of hell, less obvious but not less real, is the quiet agony of extreme individualism, the silent terror of spiritual separation from all other humans, the creeping horror of solitary mental confinement, utter isolation, complete aloneness.

Too much loneliness, for example, produces marriage — and too little produces divorce; a little of both — the happy medium — is productive partnership.

The hell of extreme individualism (you might call it " the hell of loneliness ") has been exactly pictured by C. S. Lewis in his book *The Great Divorce*. Hell, he said, is peopled by persons completely encircled with self. The longer a man is in hell, the farther he finds himself from every other human. Lewis, a typical Britisher, placed Napoleon in hell — where Dante, a devout Catholic, placed many a pope! Bonaparte, in hell only a hundred years, was already a million miles from his nearest neighbor, walking up and down (hand in vest) in a brilliantly lighted ballroom — blaming the Germans for his dismal downfall at Waterloo. In simple speech, hell is intellectual separation from the community of the living, the blackout of the ability to communicate; it is solitary self-imprisonment in a cell of loneliness.

Lewis' view plays havoc with Irvin Cobb's remark: he knew he was going to hell, he said, but he didn't mind too much; although the climate wasn't so good, the company was better. That's just the hell of it — there isn't any company!

The hell of immediate concern is precisely the one before death — the one we cause in others and ourselves! Both Lewis and Cobb (directly or indirectly) were describing a tragedy that occurs in life when an individual, insisting on his peculiar uniquity, withdraws more and more from his fellow men, locks himself in his own tomb, his own tower of silence, till he can no longer hear others speaking or understand them when he hears, till he can no longer make himself heard when he speaks. Physical withdrawal has nothing to do with it; Robinson Crusoe, for example, kept alive his contact with the human world, the community of minds, by reading the King James Bible and the English Prayer Book. Physical aloneness is restful, even curative — hence our need for prayer. Not physical aloneness, but mental aloofness is hell — the view that "I am the only intelligent person in the world, the only one worth speaking to." A man may be physically close (even too close) to thousands — in an office building, a factory, or a dormitory — yet separated from them mentally by thick soundproof glass. As though he had a contagious disease, he is isolated, not by a doctor's orders but by his own, particularly his own habit of mind. It is he who has built the padded cell that imprisons him: he can reach no one; no one can reach him. Descent into the well of loneliness, and ascent out of it, involve the same four steps: today a decision, tomorrow a habit, the third day a character, the fourth day a destiny.

There is one good thing about the hell of loneliness: as Nels Ferré has insisted, its entrance is also its exit; the man inside need not remain. Nothing is keeping him. The door is locked, to be sure, but the lock is on the inside; he locked it himself; therefore, if he will, he can unlock it — and walk out into the sunshine. It may not be easy to switch mental habits in midstream, but it is possible. Fortunately, while there's life, there's hope. Sometimes, however, a man puts off a change of mental habits (like a change of clothes) too long; the ability to change can atrophy. Conceivably a man may reach the point where his hands are paralyzed; the door to life can be opened, but the will to open it is gone. As though in a deep dark dungeon, he is sealed off effectively from the world of humans — in living death.

I have no wish to labor the point, but according to Pitirim Sorokin, habitual mental self-isolation is the determining cause of suicide. He calls it "psychosocial loneliness." You don't have to be alone to develop it; the disease is most malignant in a crowd. There are people all around you; you can even speak to them about the weather or television or the latest headline; you simply cannot talk to them, or they to you, about anything that matters (for example, about life and its meaning — that is, about religion). Psychosocial loneliness develops naturally when an individual overaccents his individuality, refuses to participate, and holds himself mentally "incommunicado." At the present state of half knowledge, it is impossible to say whether what is called "insanity" is the cause or the effect of continued self-isolation from one's fellow men.

I have an idea that psychosocial loneliness is, in fact, a major malady in our time. Crowds abound. You are always in a crowd — except in church, where the things that matter most ought to be, and are, discussed, where you don't have to apologize for mentioning (in public) such elemental items as death and life and truth. Through television the crowd is always with you — in your home. Noisy knuckleheads, selling cigarettes, beer, and laxatives, pound your tympanum from morning to midnight. If one appeared at your door and insisted on going through his idiotic spiel, you'd bury him in quicklime under the back porch, and any right-minded judge would call it justifiable homicide. Five per cent of current television is worth watching, fifteen per cent is cultural bubble gum, and the rest is a "tale told by an idiot, full of sound and fury, signifying nothing"— prepared by, and for, vacuum-packed bird brains. Too, the population is now increasing at an alarming rate; we may be three-deep on this planet in another hundred years. Crowds are not likely to decrease (except through famine, pestilence, or war). As the crowd increases, psychosocial loneliness or mental illness also increases. We talk, prattle, and chat more and more but communicate less and less; the less we have to say the longer we rattle on. It is possible that our ability to communicate, even the divine gift of speech, which distinguishes us as men, in time may disappear altogether — through lack of intelligent use!

It would not be at all strange if our century of noise, our century of crowds, were remembered in history as the age of individualism, the age of loneliness, the age of isolation, when every man not only sat under his own vine and fig tree but grew together with them, became one with them, cut off from mental contact with every other human!

Stop for a moment and ask yourself, " With how many persons now living can I talk at length or at all on any serious subject? " Have we not already reached an advanced stage of solipsism (extreme individualism) with every man in a world of his own, apart from all other men? A " cloud of unknowing " already exists between any two of us, even between closest friends, and between members of the same family! In a sense, we are *now* in hell, in mental self-isolation from one another. Fortunately, there is no guarantee that we will stay as we are. We ourselves shut the door of mental or human fellowship, and we can open it again. Nothing actually prevents us from rejoining the *human* race. One way to do it is to read the Bible, to hold a lively conversation, in agreement or disagreement, with the " thinking *humans* " who wrote it!

What is insanity? A nationally known psychiatrist stated recently that the word is no longer used by specialists in the field — that is, the so-called insane man is not insane but " incommunicado "! If he were totally devoid of sanity, of rationality, no effort to reach him would avail. His situation is this: in reaction to a severe challenge, he has dodged or ducked into a bomb shelter, and is in no hurry to come out. He has simply withdrawn from his fellow men and at the moment has no keen interest in returning to them; he has created a secure world in his imagination, and

dwells there in perpetual peace — or like the horny-eyed armadillo leers out at his imagined pursuers — at an increasing dis-
tance from all other minds. He is not insane; he has simply re-
tired from life — temporarily or permanently. The psychiatrist
and the patient are like Stanley and Livingstone; someone has to
go in after the sick man — all the way into the dark continent of
the mind withdrawn. It is not easy to find and reason with the
man, to restore his confidence that the outer world is worth re-
visiting, and, if possible, to lead him back to civilization, communication, fellowship.

Extreme individualism clearly characterizes the mentally dis-
turbed; forms of it, however, characterize also the people called
normal. They, too, lose the power to communicate unless they ex-
ercise it — on subjects deeper than the weather.

An important difference can be observed between Jesus and the
Essenes, who also were teachers in his day: they remained in their
monastic community, withdrawn from the world; Jesus was not
content to be cut off from his fellow men. Out he went to them,
while the Essenes frowned. He traveled up and down the highways and byways of Galilee, Samaria, and Judea, even to Gentile
Tyre and Sidon, making contact with lonely folk, ending their
loneliness. Each Gospel story stresses the aloneness, the spiritual
isolation, of the people to whom he ministered; he journeyed deep
into their private mental jungles, their private mental hells, and
brought them again to the light (what Dante called Christ's
"harrowing of hell"). Sometimes the needy ones came to him,
but only because he first had come to them.

The goal of all life is holy communion, holy community — the
meeting of mind with mind, in your home, on your street, and
across the width of the world. Communion in itself *is* holy, wherever you find it — and in whatever form; Jesus said that where
two commune in his name, he is present; where two commune
in any name God is present. Thieves commune, it is true, to hurt
and destroy; good men commune to heal and build — which
means simply that there is power, good power, in communion, to
be used or abused. On Paul's terms, the married communion of

body with body is also holy, and the bed undefiled. Human beings
were made by and for communion, and without it wither and
die. Unfortunately, bread and wine are more common than holy
communion in the sacrament of the Lord's Supper, for holy communion is the meeting of minds (not necessarily their agreement). The extreme individual, the island dweller, has lost the
power to commune, is out of touch with the human race. He sits
within his darkened mind and tells himself a lie. " I don't need
anyone," he says. " All I want is to be left alone." In the office of
Beloit psychologist Lester E. Wiley, a wall cartoon presents a
sour-looking chap sitting back in a box, thinking to himself:
" People are no damn good! " The sour-looking chap naïvely imagines the statement includes everyone but himself. He has the
mind of the horny-eyed armadillo leering out at the world.

One thing only (namely, holy communion) can overcome negative individualism, the hell of loneliness. It is the Holy Spirit
that " does not love a wall." " By faith the walls of Jericho fell
down." (Heb. 11:30, RSV.) It is the Holy Spirit that heals every
schism in the body of mankind, that pulls down the wall of separation between the sacred and the secular, between Jew and Gentile. For this reason, the walking Holy Communion, the walking
Holy Spirit — Jesus — reached out and included lonely island
dwellers, ended their inward isolation, restored them to sanity
and community.

All of us, I suppose, need to get away from people now and
then — but not to stay. You don't have to be a cannibal to get
" fed up " with people. Nonetheless, far more than we realize, it
is just people that we need — all kinds of people, and they are all
here; we actually need the people who annoy us, the people who
irritate us, the people who see through us and dislike us. They
keep our feet on the ground; they keep us in living contact with
the human world; without them, we might lose touch altogether!
Fénelon, a saint who managed to remain one at the court of
Louis XIV, was less than saintly when he said, " Hardly one ob-
noxious person goeth away, before another cometh." We all feel
that way at times. But the attitude is its own damnation. People

who sneer at other people, said Jesus, are in danger of hell-fire (Matt. 5:22, RSV), indeed, are already aflame with it. For example, faculty frowners sometimes say, "The masses cannot think; they are interested only in bread and sex." People who look down at other people are automatically self-isolated, automatically in hell. C. S. Lewis said that you can't at one and the same moment look down in contempt at your neighbor, and up in humility at God. Smart people who look down at dumb people aren't very smart after all, or they would know that they, too, are dumb.

The Pharisee in Jesus' parable was a pious snob, that is, a prig. (Luke 18:10 f., RSV.) The woods, the churches, and fraternal organizations, are full of this species of bug. According to Jesus, the Pharisee's pride of piety had isolated him from the human race. He thought he had excluded them; he had merely excluded himself. His words sound exactly like today's negative individual, living in his own padded cell away from holy communion.

In effect, Jesus told the story this way: "Two men went up into the temple to pray, the one a prig, and the other a pub owner. The prig stood and prayed thus with himself (no one else was listening, apparently not even God): 'I thank thee that I am not as other men — numskulls, democrats, integrationists, one-worlders, Negroes, Jews, Englishmen, and communists. I neither smoke, drink, nor chew — nor associate with women who do. I move fast twice a week — when I go to collect the rents. Every year I give five dollars to the church and ten to the United Givers — then take a full ten per cent deduction on my Federal Income Tax.' But the pub owner, standing afar off, would not lift up so much as his eyes unto heaven, but smote upon his breast, saying: 'O God, your son was born in a pub owner's barn — maybe you can find room in your heart for me. And don't be too hard on the Pharisee; he's not a bad fellow really; he means well; trouble is, he sometimes gets all closed up in himself.'" Jesus then commented somewhat like this: "I tell you, the pub owner went down to his house justified, rather than the prig, for everyone that exalteth himself shall have few friends (on earth or in heaven), but he that humbleth himself shall have many!"

7

The " Romantic " Protestant

The romantic Protestant (anemic caricature of the original) is the man who says, " It makes no difference what you believe — one belief is as good as another." The rational Protestant is the man who says, " Some beliefs make all the difference in the world; for example, in democracy as against dictatorship, in freedom as against slavery, in equal justice as against racial (or any other) segregation, in sense as against nonsense in belief itself, and finally in life-centered as against death-centered religion." These beliefs have marked man's slow ascent from primeval slime to the Sermon on the Mount; the same beliefs will mark man's continued climb toward civilized spirituality and spiritualized civilization.

Protestantism began as a revolt against lack of thought; it did not advocate the wishy-washy empty mind — the head that wobbles with every wind. The Reformers found in Rome's frozen finalities a complete mental blackout; they insisted that rational thought be returned to the Christian church (from its long exile in outer light), that intellectual honesty cut away the encrusted accumulation of priestly hocus-pocus. The Reformation, for a time, reunited reason and religion (too long in separate residences); it thus started something as yet not wholly stopped, something that can never really be stopped, for honest thinking, the presence and thrust of the Holy Spirit, is more than an occasional necessity. When the grandchildren of Protestant pioneers have achieved the *romantic,* vacant mind, the holy cause of rational religion, Protestantism, has run, like a river, into the desert, and there disappeared.

One thing for sure about Luther: he was not a romantic Protestant, a balloon or bubblehead; he was an egghead. The egg hatched a rational revolution — the duty of the individual to think for himself, to learn to distinguish relevant from irrelevant religion, life from death. Luther knew what he was talking about; he had been raised in Roman legalism, fully absorbed in what he later regarded as the concentrated superstition, the colossal miscarriage, the organized blackmail called Catholicism. Like Saul the Pharisee, who became Paul the Christian philosopher, Luther the Augustinian lamb became the lion of the Reformation. But first he had given Catholicism thirty years of firm and full obedience; he had outdone others and himself in impeccable faithfulness to Rome's endless trivia. He had accepted the whole bag of tricks, tried them all out, and kept at them — like a Buddhist turning a prayer wheel, or a squirrel in a cage. Monastic education, as he experienced it, was mostly monkey see, monkey do.

However, before as well as after his intellectual awakening, he took religious truth seriously — as worth a struggle to find, and a struggle to keep. Like Buddha before the Bo-tree, he had nearly killed himself — denying and depriving his own body. Further, he had gone beyond other monks in probing the foundations of Roman faith. He spoke not as a noisy ignoramus, but as a not-so-quiet expert, when he said: " I do not accept the authority of popes and councils, for they have contradicted each other. . . . Unless I am convinced by Scripture and plain reason — I cannot and I will not recant anything. . . . The pope is no judge of matters pertaining to God's Word and faith, but the Christian man must examine and judge for himself." Luther discovered what it is to think, to think honestly, to think without fear, without mental subservience to political or religious secret police. He broke through to the simple, wonderful joy of being, for the first time, a man, a child of God, a thinking human — in principle inwardly free from every form of bondage. He recognized thinking as man's primary link with God — at once a privilege and a duty. Hence, he would accept nothing from church or state unless honestly convinced that it was true. In effect he nailed ninety-five arguments to every church door, challenging the world to public and permanent debate, in order that popular beliefs of all kinds might be sifted for their root value.

Unless a particular belief or set of beliefs can convince intellectual integrity, it cannot be accepted by responsible men. Where the romantic Protestant announces with a wave of his hand, " One belief is as good as another," Luther, a rational Protestant, was willing, if need be, to be burned at the stake (like John Hus before him) rather than allow the stupid tyranny of sacred superstition, with its stranglehold on freedom of faith, to go unchallenged!

The most important thing, the most defining thing, about any man is what he believes; false belief, however, curses and cripples the mind; only what is true, said Jesus, sets men free. Not his bank roll or his union card, not his political or religious affiliation, but what a man honestly thinks — this is his measure; this is the man! The rest is transportation and reproduction. Moved by the Holy Spirit, Luther fought the holy battle of reason, the will of God, in religion; he did not say, " It makes no difference what you believe."

Chesterton, I think, was half right; he said, " Tolerance is the virtue of people who don't believe anything " — that is, by definition, romantic Protestants. There is, of course, a creative tolerance; perhaps our age could teach Luther a thing or two about it. We are learning, at snail's pace, that if we want the right to believe as honest thinking dictates, we must grant the same right to every man and every religion. It is possible that this point is clearer today than in the sixteenth century. However, if we fail to see what Luther saw, we were not only born blind, but have remained the blind who lead or the blind who follow! One thing we are in danger of losing: the conviction of Luther, and of Buddha, that right belief is a matter of life and death, worth losing an eye or a hand to find, worth hunting and dying for — that generations yet to come may live not in darkness but in light, not in fear but in freedom!

Modern liberalism has taught us a few lessons we will do well to remember: for example, to leave room somewhere in our thinking for the reality that is greater than our thought. God's truth is more than our truth; for this reason we refrain, as best we can, from killing, crippling, or excommunicating folk who disagree with us; they may have a little right and a little wrong in their belief — as we do. After all, liberalism learned this lesson the hard way through centuries of religious fanaticism — of vindictiveness, acrimony, and bloodletting. To forget this lesson is to take again the consecrated knife, to bind the world's children, like Isaac, upon the alters of conformist sacrifice. Recently we passed through an un-American fever of fanaticism. It could happen again.

However, we cannot afford to overlook another lesson from liberalism itself. A blackout of honest thinking is not tolerance but idiocy — feeble-minded ineptitude. The great liberals thought long and hard to locate a modest measure of truth. To them it made all the difference in the world whether or not their beliefs were true, for example, whether the earth is round or flat, whether the earth or the sun is the center of our solar system, whether a man has or has not the right to think freely, without penalty, regardless of approval or disapproval by church or state. Galileo, Copernicus, and Newton would feel small sympathy with the romantic Protestant view that anything goes in the world of belief, that superstition is as good as rational faith, that magic is as good as meaning and medicine, that human sacrifice (killing people) is as good as human service. It seems likely that the great liberals would regard many of us, their descendants, as effeminate surface dwellers — intellectual milksops, nincompoops, nonentities.

Romantic Protestantism is decadent individualism — individualism gone to seed. It seeks cowardly escape from the toughness of intellectual struggle, combat, pilgrimage. It says in effect: "African mumbo jumbo is as valuable as medical science; incantation is as helpful as penicillin; witch-burning is more natural, and more exciting, than the right to be different; slavery, especially the slavery of the mind, is as legitimate as freedom of thought."

True, our forefathers sometimes made asses of themselves in public, arguing heatedly and at length over matters that seem to us peripheral at best and piffle at worst. In this regard, you and I often prove in action our true paternity. In Lexington, Kentucky, in front of the Union Terminal, you will find a metal plaque bearing the legend that on or near that spot, a hundred years ago, with Henry Clay as chairman, Alexander Campbell and another clergyman debated for two solid weeks about the necessity of baptism by immersion as a means to salvation. Of course, an important issue (though seldom mentioned) was at stake beneath the hue and cry: immersion as superstition, as a substitute for helpful living, or immersion as an optional outward sign of inward ethical reconstruction. In other words, is baptism, in any form (for other than sanitary reasons), important in its own right or a mere signpost or arrow pointing to something else, something wholly different, something really important — a new mind, a mind set to find and practice what is true. No such debate, I think, could occur today. The romantic Protestant has taken over; to him there are no issues important enough to be worth debating. Both his God and himself are too nice to argue. Both prefer slippers and the peace pipe of capitulation; both, it seems, would rather believe a lie than resist one.

It boils down to this: are a man's beliefs, a man's thoughts and convictions, of central and pivotal importance? Karl Marx thought so; to him, it made all the difference in the world whether a man did, or did not, *think* like a communist. Is the essential man, or is he not, what he thinks? The modern pseudo-liberal considers matters of belief of no consequence one way or another; he seems to be the real atheist of our generation: in his view, man has lost his one distinction from the chimpanzee, his primary link with God — his capacity for thinking, for discerning truth from error. On these terms, modern man is not merely an orphan; he is a vacuum, a hollow man, a busy mechanic; he has no inner history and no upper story. The body remains; the thinking mind (the glory) has departed. The brain has gone soft; all you have left is legs.

It made a difference to Clarence Darrow, and indeed to William Jennings Bryan, whether the earth was created in six twenty-four-hour days or six billion years. Bryan was out to defend the faith he had received as a family heirloom; his emotions were bound up with it. Darrow was out to clear the air, to let God's sunlight into closed religious devotion. To both men, it made a difference whether Americans believed sense or nonsense; both were willing to make a loud noise in public about it. Today, our loud public noises largely concern the latest development in baseball, football, or tiddlywinks — and mass lip service to a mild form of the faith of the Middle Ages in Madison Square Garden.

We don't shout, we whisper, about the mass denial of equal human rights in Northern real estate and Southern religion. It is not at all settled and certain whether men will be free to think, tomorrow and the day after, or forced to submit to political and religious brainwashing; it is not at all a foregone conclusion, as yet, whether men in the immediate future will evolve further toward divine Sonship or retreat from faith to fear, from standing erect in sunlight to crouching in Plato's cave.

It is obvious, of course, as liberalism has taught us, that the same truth may be stated in different ways, different languages, different religions; no doubt the romantic Protestant intends to champion this important insight. Whether men call on the name of Jehovah, Allah, or the Universe, for example, is less important than doing the will of God; injustice smells in any language. The universe is what it is, regardless of our thought about it, in any religion. Among Buddhists and Christians alike, half the people believe in better life above life or after death — the other half believe in *better life* (and labor with love to achieve it). In both religions you are confronted with similar alternatives. Only the culture, clothing, language, and ritual differ. Within either religion, however, it makes all the difference in the world whether men seek holy communion for the few withdrawn from life and after death — or whole communion for the many in life. In either re-

ligion, it makes a difference whether imagination or illusion cap-
tures, and holds, human attention!

I have my doubts about Jesus crouching against a wall and cry-
ing for Calvary — in a modern city or anywhere — but I'm reasonably certain he would not be content to have his ethic of equal
justice neither damned nor defended. Perhaps he foresaw the
sterility, the neither hot nor cold, of the romantic Protestant,
when he asked, " When the Son of man comes, will he find faith
on the earth? "

It made a difference to Lincoln whether the American Negro
should be set free or remain a slave. Today efforts are sometimes
made to buy and sell the Negro's vote, but not the Negro. All of
us have heard dozens of plausible reasons why Lincoln signed
the Emancipation Proclamation; many ulterior motives and self-
interested objectives have been alleged — to give Northern big
business a shot in the arm, to aid the prosecution of the war by
turning slaves against their masters, or the simple lust for personal publicity (in history books!). Southerners, at least, seldom
agree — God bless them! They usually suspect Lincoln of whole-
sale commitment to the " equal rights " heresy. Will cynics forgive me if I consider Lincoln guilty as charged? I can't prove it,
but I believe he sweat great drops of blood over the issue, that he
thought long and hard about it before he came to power, and for
three years as President. Not easily could he bring himself to
strike so big a blow for brotherhood!

Both North and South have a problem, a very real problem; the
problem is the question, What is man? It makes all the difference
in the world whether a human being is, or is not, entitled to be
treated like one. Americans were sensitive about human rights in
1776 when they started a war to gain and maintain those rights
(for themselves). Americans were sensitive about equal rights
when they defended the French against the Kaiser, all Europe
against Hitler, and all Korea against the Kremlin. For some reason, we were noticeably less sensitive about equal rights for North
American Indians, and today have something less than a frenzy
of enthusiasm about equal rights for Negroes. We have a way to

go to become human, even to find out what a human being is. We have a way to go to achieve the better life for all our fellow earth dwellers. Only the way to hell is paved with good intentions. As T. S. Eliot has understood, here, whether or not hereafter, the alternative to hell is not heaven but purgatory — for climbing is cleansing on the way to community. Progress is made for all, but only *by* thinking persons to whom the belief in equal human dignity makes a difference worth shouting about — " who more than self their country *loved,* And mercy [or just plain justice] more than life! " It takes courage to evolve.

When you hear an adult say: " It makes no difference what men believe," you can put it down that (temporarily at least) he has leaped all the way from adolescence to senility. The world is made, not for spineless nonentities, for men with brains like sofa pillows, but for heroes, for heroes make the world a community of *minds.* " Stand therefore," said Paul, " having your loins girt about with truth." (Eph. 6:14, KJV.)

8

Capitalism with Compassion

There is, after all, a difference between uncreative and creative capitalism, a difference often ignored by strong defenders and strong accusers alike. The difference is the presence or absence of constructive compassion, the healing realism, the Holy Spirit — for the truest form of human thinking is Love. As Paul could be rephrased: now abideth political faith and economic hope, but greater than these is maturity.

Capitalism cannot be identified with Christianity, but can be an expression of it. Communism tends to sacrifice personal freedom in its haste to achieve economic brotherhood; it makes the individual a means, and the group the end. Capitalism, at times, is the exact reverse: it sacrifices the common well-being to personal self-advancement; it makes the good of all secondary to the good of one. It is important, however, to realize that self-centered capitalism is not the whole of it.

Honesty is more productive than a party line. Also, as Lecomte du Noüy put it: it is better to be generous than just. A distinguished clergyman said to me one day: " Why don't you call capitalism by its right name — larceny? " Well, capitalism and larceny are sometimes identical, but not always — and perhaps less often than you think. The salary of the distinguished clergyman, and the maintenance of his church, come entirely from the giving and self-giving of people who work for profit — corporation managers, stockholders, and white- or blue-collar laborers. As a college professor, I sometimes remember that colleges are maintained by people who work for money — including college professors.

Uncreative capitalism, I think, can be accurately described as larceny — though legal, subtle, and respectable. Capitalism without compassion is also capitalism without ethical competition. In theory, every man has the right to start an enterprise, no matter how many persons or corporations are already in the field; in practice, new business ventures are not only not encouraged, but are actually often pushed to the wall by cutthroat chicanery parading as "free enterprise." A wolf is a wolf — even when disguised as Red Ridinghood's grandmother; and a loan shark is a loan shark — however vigorously he shouts, "Liberty!" and waves American flags in Fourth-of-July celebrations. Not a little American business, both large and small, does, in fact, operate on the philosophy: "Get him — before he gets you!" Part, at least, of our American business "community" is as cozy as an African jungle — or a South Chicago gang war.

A friend of mine worked for a time — as long as he could stand it — as an insurance claims adjuster in Brooklyn. His job, as he describes it, was simply fleecing the insured. Every day his boss, himself under pressure from higher-ups (from bigger crocodiles with larger mouths and longer tails), would say to him, "In the present case, the insured is entitled to a four-hundred-dollar settlement; talk him into accepting two hundred dollars instead — or don't come back!" In careful training sessions, he learned exactly how to hoodwink a client — first with smiles and kindness, second with gentle threats, and finally with a whole assortment of low blows and dirty tricks. The client, ill and out of work, was thus forced to accept half or a quarter of the cash settlement to which he was legally entitled — for which he had paid through the nose for years on end. Capitalists of this sort are like rats gnawing corpses in a graveyard.

However, all the obvious miscarriage and malodorous larceny notwithstanding, a creative capitalism is among us also; further, it is much more common than many realize. Not everyone works to rob his fellow men. In actual practice, few do. Most folk I know work every day in part for the love of the work, in part to feed and educate their families, and in part to provide a little fun now and then on the side. In simple fact, do you know anyone who doesn't? Even in Russia, people work because they like to work, but also for pay — as we do! You might call them "communist capitalists."

Creative capitalism, then, is capitalism with compassion — steady and steadily constructive! It is the quiet and unsung altruism of a man supporting his family in good times and bad times for fifty years, all the time doing his best to avoid sacrificing other people's interests to his own, all the time finding room in his slender income for his church and for all sorts of charities — now and then indulging wildly in a little nondeductible giving to a neighbor in need.

It would actually shock some folk I know to learn that they too are capitalists. For example, a college professor, as we have suggested, is a capitalist; he works for the love of the work, but also for a salary check. Neither would be any good without the other. You say, "But the professor has no capital." I disagree; he has crammed more information than other men (some of it, we hope, correct) into his cranium. He has, so to speak, something of a corner on his special kind of knowledge. If people want it, they have to come to him for it. He is usually a poor bargainer or he would get a better price for it. The average professor's salary in this country is exactly equal to the average floor sweeper's salary in the better factories. Nonetheless, the professor (you might call him a faculty mind sweeper), like the factory floor sweeper, works for profit as well as for public improvement. The same is true of clergymen, evangelists, missionaries, doctors, lawyers, merchants, priests — along with plumbers, ditchdiggers, and house painters.

It should be remembered that Jesus was a kind of capitalist: as a carpenter he worked for the love of the work (his yokes were easy) but also for pay; later he launched a new enterprise (to set a light glowing in the minds of men) and was pushed to the wall by unethical, monopolistic competition. He worked for the joy of the work (the Bible says so again and again), but also to feed and clothe his disciples and their families. The cross, to be sure, was poor remuneration for three years of public service; it has proved profitable enough, but for us, not for him. However, Jesus is not the only creative worker who ran afoul of conservatism — and received evil for good.

As I see it, creative capitalism has four positive ideas. Without these ideas, the world would be poor indeed. First, personal freedom to think and act is to be preserved (by ethical competition — if necessary at legal gun point) and encouraged, against every form of monopoly or social tyranny. Second, work for the love of the work is true art — that is, to a good workman his work is his play, his prayer, and his psychiatry, for a happy worker is a happy man. Third, people are more important than profits. Fourth, a man's true measure is not what he takes, and not what he makes, but what he gives — of himself!

First: creative capitalism takes freedom seriously and defends it against every form of monopoly, whether economic, political, or religious. A monopoly, even a religious monopoly, is neither more nor less than an economic dictatorship maintained by moral or physical force. Democracy in economics means every man's right to start an enterprise of his own — no matter how many predatory or laudatory corporations already claim the field. Further, every man is entitled to ethical competition — tough enough in itself. Even more, every man is entitled to be lent a hand or two now and then to help him get his show on the road. I saw what happens in communist countries where official government monopolies run everything — there was not much choice of things to buy, and all of them poor grade. You may be a little short on Sputniks, but you do have more and better mousetraps when no man is denied the right to try to make a better one than his neighbor.

Unthinking people sometimes ask: "Why are there so many denominations? Why not have just one big church — so nobody would have to exert himself to support it?" The answer is obvious. You either do or do not have democracy in religion; to have it means you grant your neighbor the right to start a new

religious enterprise (even a new denomination) if he feels so inclined — the same right your forefathers insisted on when they
started yours. Would you rather have someone stand over every
new religious venture with a club — to beat it into the ground?
That was standard procedure in the Catholic Middle Ages; mod-
ified only a little it is also standard procedure in today's Catholic
Spain, and in Catholic or Spanish South America. Co-operation
and amalgamation are fine; we are moving slowly in that direction; nonetheless, if everyone is forced into one political party or
one church, democracy is dead. When that happens, Luther lived
in vain, and John Hus in vain was burned at the stake.

You either do, or do not, believe in economic freedom, including international freedom of trade. Creative capitalism usually
does believe in it — for the same reason it believes in freedom of
faith.

Second: work done with an eye to work well done is an art,
whether the work is garbage-collecting or mural-painting. A lot
of people will tell you they don't like to work. That's merely a
standard conversation piece, an invitation to dialogue. The fact is,
I have never known anyone who didn't like to work, though I
have known a few, some in advanced years, who hadn't found
the work they wanted to do. It's true, of course: if you can't get
the job you like, like the job you get. Work is a necessity for mental health — and for physical health as well. Work gives you a
feeling of belonging, of having someone depend on you for something, of not quite living in vain. People who retire too early have
to take up some enterprise — or die, from the mind down, of
simple boredom.

I can't really understand the chap who is bursting for a fifty-
year vacation at Miami Beach — along with the other jellyfish cast
up by the sea. I like a little relaxation, a little fun, every day —
but vacations, unless combined with speechmaking or book-writ-
ing, bore me to tears. In fact, I find one job a rest from another.
When I tire of teaching college students, I write a book. When I
tire of writing a book, I hunt up a congregation and preach.
When I tire of preaching, I teach college students, etc. When I tire

of all three, or all three tire of me, I turn my mind off altogether and watch television — like any self-respecting American moron.

Young people under thirty, who haven't quite found themselves, sometimes feel that money is more important than work. For this reason, a few take the short cut called crime — which leads nowhere. They nurse a secret hatred of work itself, and of all people who work; they yearn to be corporation executives — to smoke fifty-cent cigars and cultivate the corporation under their belts. We all have to pass through a troubled period of finding ourselves. Most people past thirty, however, have made their work their play — or they are dead! They would rather do a good piece of work (morally and emotionally satisfying) than rot mentally on Miami Beach. They are not simon-pure philanthropists, of course: that is, they keep an eye on the salary check — when no one is looking. They are even willing to shout and gripe a little, now and then, to help the check gain weight! But you can't say they work only for money. It's more the other way around; the money works for them; it enables them to do the work they want to do.

Third: creative capitalism, moved by compassion, the Holy Spirit, usually remembers that people are not made for profits, but profits for people. When profits are considered more important than people, socialism or communism is not far away, an inevitable reaction to the basic insult offered human dignity. I'm an unreconstructed Jeffersonian myself: the nation governs best that governs least. More nations have been destroyed by top-heavy governments than by foreign armies. Internal barbarians (in and out of office) are more to be feared than the descendants of Genghis Khan! However, the less government or self-government there is *inside* men (and corporations), the more there must be *outside*. In simple words: if working capitalism is without effective compassion, without respect for people above respect for profits, stronger governments are inevitable — to resist the economic Hitlers. If profit seekers (whether labor unions or manufacturers) do not practice self-restraint, someone must and will restrain them. This means, in the long run, that capitalists have a choice

— to practice the principle that people are more important than profits, or lose capitalism itself to socialism or communism. When brotherhood (by law if not by grace) is cast into outer darkness, freedom (the Siamese twin) usually follows it in no great length of time.

The cure, to be sure, is worse than the disease, for communism, which crusades in the name of the people, normally ends by suppressing the people altogether. But the cause, the root of communism — let us face it — is uncreative capitalism, capitalism without compassion, without ethical competition, capitalism which prefers profits to people. Three hundred years ago (for example) a British owner of a tobacco plantation in Virginia was asked about the souls of his workers; he replied, "Damn their souls, let them raise tobacco!"

Finally, creative capitalism, the child of holy compassion, knows all the time that the true measure of a man is not what he makes or takes but what he gives. People are paid widely different salaries for all sorts of reasons. Prize fighters make more money in a single fight than college presidents make all their lives, which appears to mean that rank-and-file Americans value the muscles they share with the ox and the ass above the minds they share with scientists and saints. A vacuum-brained nonentity with a voice like pancake syrup makes more money in one television appearance than Albert Schweitzer has ever seen — he builds hospitals with less. This is called the American standard of values. But the alternative is to have somebody tell us all (at the point of a gun) how much we shall receive for our services, and there's a shortage of people and committees we would all be willing to trust. For the present at least — unless things get too bad — we would rather let the public pay us what it thinks we're worth than leave the decision to a Washington expert.

Not what you make but what you give — this is your measure, the measure of what is inside you, the measure of your mind. Albert Schweitzer has made little, but given much — and, come to think of it, Americans value him too! Perhaps, in point of fact, Americans do prefer full brains to fullbacks after all! In any case, before God, before man, and before yourself, you are what you give — and neither more nor less. For this reason, Jews and Christians have always insisted on setting apart not less than ten per cent of their earnings for causes beyond the narrow circle of self-concern. A few glorious souls, just to show it can be done, have lived on ten per cent and given ninety per cent to public enrichment. Schools and colleges thus endowed are designed to keep people from superstition and fear, to train them to contribute skillfully to the common good; churches thus supported are designed to increase effective compassion in common capitalists (like you and me); hospitals are designed to help average citizens stay mentally and physically mobile. All three enterprises (and thousands more) owe their existence and their maintenance, not to chance charity, not to paternalism, not to almsgiving, not even to capitalist larceny — but simply and steadily to capitalism with compassion, perpetually among us, the actual source of whatever strength we have, in some real degree uniting the Holy Spirit and the human spirit.

Creative capitalism knows, deep down, that the way of constructive compassion, constructive realism, is the way of victory for all; that nations are weakened by slavery but strengthened by freedom; that work for the love of the work, and for profit, does not impoverish but enriches the total economy; that to value people above profits is the righteousness that exalts a nation; that giving beyond mere making and taking creates and sustains both dignity and community. Continually to work and continually to give, said Jesus, this is what God has always done in his faithfulness toward us. According to Genesis, the Almighty himself worked a six-day week; yet he seeks, on the seventh day also, the increase of his own constructive compassion in us all. And now abideth faith in work and hope of gain, but greater than these is self-giving. (I Cor. 13:13, paraphrase.)

9

One God, One Universe, One Community

What God in the universe seems to be saying to us is this: "My children, there is much unfinished in you, individually and collectively, outwardly and inwardly; you are not very bright; you haven't evolved very far, as yet, from the dust of the ground — but I love you and will sustain you. I have brought you thus far and will bring you the rest of the way. I have sworn to complete what I have begun. Nothing can stop me; nothing can separate you from my love. Fear not, for I am with you; despair not, for I am God; I will strengthen you; I will help you; I will defend you (not too much but enough!) from the enemy without and the enemy within." (Isa. 41:10, paraphrase.)

God is not only our call to growth in love; he is not only our clear-eyed critic; he is also our unity and community, our everlasting comfort — our friend, counselor, and guide. We have never walked alone; we are never alone. There is a gospel as well as a clap of thunder in creative religion, and the good news is this: a strength and wisdom more than human now sustain, and will sustain, the total human pilgrimage, and each individual pilgrim all the way to world community and personal maturity.

You might put it this way: not man alone, but God, over, under, and in each man and all kinds of men, is the architect and the engineer of community. We have our assigned tasks, and they are socially and personally important, but a hand more experienced than our own is at work around us and in us *all* (Africans, Chinese, Russians, and Americans alike!) Our idiocies can delay a world of productive peace; they can prevent neither its appearance nor its permanence. Our stupidities can delay the increase of Christ in every individual; this, too, they cannot prevent — for God is God, the Almighty. The gates of hell, said Jesus, cannot withstand, cannot resist, the thrust of the Holy Spirit. (Matt. 16:18, paraphrase.) We are on our way toward world fellowship, an international neighborhood, a community of sanity on this earth — embracing all men in all lands, languages, and religions — " a city which hath foundations, whose builder and maker is God."

Beyond the collective unconscious, and beyond self-centered individualism, community begins where love begins, and love begins with a thankful heart — not alone for prosperity, which can get in our way, not alone for health of mind and body, or wealth of freedom, but for God himself, our one constant source and resource, our one fountain of blessing from whom has come, and will keep coming, the Age of Man (already more than a dwarf), the Age of Reason, the Age of the Spirit. The Kingdom of Heaven is ahead, but it is also up, down, and all around; it is here, and here to stay — for God is here! He is author of the treasure that neither moth nor rust can corrupt, nor thieves nor governments break through and steal.

History, I think, will show that the dawn of the Age of the Sputnik was also the dawn of the New Age of the Spirit — of seven-league strides toward world community, of healing sanity released in the minds of men from the mind of God. For man receives and distorts community; its creator and author is God. From on high, so to speak, mankind at last has been shifted out of low gear!

Thankfulness, properly understood, is not merely offered to God; it is not simply a signed receipt for blessings duly delivered; rather, thankfulness is primarily *for* God. He is both the Blesser and the Blessing, both the Giver and the Gift; it is only reality, his presence among us, that enables the discerning to face the future without fear; it is only his power and purpose among us that will be the reason for our rejoicing — tomorrow not less than yesterday and today — that is, when earthly pilgrims land on Venus, Mars, and the Moon, not less than when they landed on the far side of the Red Sea, and on Plymouth Rock! In his patience is our progress! In his dependable goodness is our peace of mind. With him beside us, what need have we of ulcers?

God is always too new and too good to be true, yet is true indeed, and truth itself! He is in the business of making big men in a big world, men big enough to walk with him and with one another in love; he is in the business of creating a community of minds — to begin with in us, and in all our fellow earth dwellers. Not for any lesser thing, however wonderful, but just for God the universe, for God himself, thinking men have thankful hearts. They understand the colored man's prayer: " O Lord, take care of yourself! If anything happens to you, we're all sunk."

The word " God " means twenty-five words (and more) to me; one day I may write more about them. The first five (Love, Power, Faithfulness, Fruitfulness, Fellowship) are reducible to one word: Community. " I will pray the Father," said Jesus, " and he shall unite you — in the Spirit of truth." (John 14:16, 17, paraphrase.) God has always been here; he has always been our call to evolution and the critic of our proud pretensions; even more, he has always been the strength and comfort of sinners and of saints. As Jesus put it: " He maketh his sun to rise on the evil and on the good, and sendeth rain on the just and on the unjust." (Matt. 5:45, KJV.) Within his care and control, within his hand, within his heart, all men (whether sinners or saints) live and move and have their being — from first to last. No one lives outside God. There is no " outside God." Because he is One, the universe is a *uni*verse. Because he is One, we are one. Because he is One, we are not divided.

We live not in evil but in good, for we dwell at this moment, always, and altogether within the House of the Lord. Though as big as all space and all time, God is no farther from any one of us than our own flesh, our own spirit, whether we are Hindus, Buddhists, Moslems, Christians, or Jews, whether ditchdiggers, scientists, or saints. All around us is God, and all around us is good. Our human injustice, our inhumanity to one another, abounds, but good even more abounds, for good is the grace of existence, the grace of life, the grace of mind — even the mind that conceives evil and brings it to birth. Evil is not good, but the mind that conceives it is good, for without the mind man conceives nothing. The mind itself is the searchlight God has set inside each of us; you might call it also the mouthpiece through which he speaks inside us the truth about his world, the truth about himself — that he is Love, that we can trust him.

Community exists and grows because God not only afflicts the too-comfortable, but also comforts the too-afflicted. Community (the meeting of minds) begins because God says to us: " My child, you are the highest order of being I have yet brought forth, but I am not at present overly proud of my handiwork. Give me a little time; the work has barely begun. At the moment you are not very much, one way or another, but I love you and will complete in you my image and likeness. I will put my heart in your heart, my mind in your mind — and no man will need say to his brother, ' Know the Lord,' for you shall all know me, from the least of you to the greatest; for the earth shall be full of true knowledge, true justice, true love, as the waters cover the sea." (Isa. 11 :9, paraphrase.)

You ask: " How can you say that all men are *now* one family in God? Wherever you look, man's hand is raised against his brother, religion is pitted against religion, and government against government." I reply: " Our divisions are secondary, our unity is primary; our conflicts are superficial, our community is basic; our disharmonies are on the surface (like the waves of the sea); our common life from and in one universe, one God, is not fiction but fact. It is reality! There have always been many religions, for a religion is a language, and there are many languages. There have been many religions, for each man (in part) has created his own, bearing his image. At the same time there has never been but one religion, the increase of the Holy Spirit in the human spirit, the growth of reason, the growth of mind; you might call it man's dance, or wrestle, with reality, with one universe, one God."

All men know him, for he is neighbor to all. No one knows him well, for we hardly know ourselves, and he is our life in body and in mind. However, there's not one of us who does not know him, not one of us who has not met him — every hour, every minute, every second, of life itself. Different men call him by different names; he has many "aliases." By whatever name he is called, his presence is the universe beneath us, the universe over us, the universe at our side, the universe in front and in back of us, the universe within. Psalm 100 says it this way: "It is he that hath made us, and not we ourselves; we are his people, and the sheep of his pasture." His hand follows us, goes before us, holds us up, holds us apart, and holds us together — when we are good, but also when we are evil; not on Sundays only, but seven days a week. His goodness toward us does not change whether we change or not; his faithfulness toward us is our courage, our confidence, and our competence; his fruitfulness within us is our growth in dignity and community. His fellowship with himself and his creatures, made clear in Christ, has always baptized both nature and man with love and power. You know him; in a sense, you know only him; he looks at you through every pair of eyes, speaks to you through every pair of lips.

And he says: "My child, you do get frightened now and then; you are always, you know, finite and fallible — and often, though not always, futile and funny. You are afraid of the dark; you love to entertain yourself with tales of ghosts and goblins; the only ghosts you have really to fight are ignorance and greed — and neither is unconquerable — for stronger than either is good, my good, even in men who are evil. No evil can outwit me — and I am with you. My rod and my staff, they comfort you. I have prepared a table before you, in the presence of your enemies; I have anointed your head with oil; your cup runneth over. Surely goodness and mercy shall follow you all the days of your life — and you shall dwell in my house, in my hand, forever."

One day, in the midst of a battle, a grinning GI shouted to a very worried chaplain: "What's the matter, Padre? Haven't you overlooked something?" "What?" snapped the hard-pressed clergyman. "God," replied the GI.

Community (the holy communion of free men, of grown men, of all men, with one another and with God) is not a human invention, not a panacea, not a quack remedy, not a dream — whether wishful or wistful. Rather, it is the structure of reality, the coherence of the universe, the Logos, the rationality, the nature of God; because it is his nature, it is also his demand; because it is his demand, it is also (when we are ready) his gift. He is now preparing us to receive it; he is now nourishing us to receive it fully! It is on the agenda of history. One thing has always been here, always coming through to us; one thing right now is coming through to us more clearly — the face of God. His presence is the fact, and the fact, every fact, is his presence; it's his presence that makes us one. Mankind is one, really one, has always been, will always be — for one universe is our Source and Sustenance. Mankind is one — and one day will learn to remember it, to rejoice in it.

Our sins are no doubt great, though we often overestimate the little ones and underestimate the big ones. The biggest one is our failure to rejoice with all men in life — our common Giver and his uncommon Gift. We love to overestimate everything about ourselves — except the one thing we can never overestimate, that God is our Father, that we are brothers under the sun. The doctrine of divine forgiveness for sins small and great, in all the religions of the world, means this: God says to us, "My son, this time, to be sure, you bobbled; this time, to be sure, you missed the boat; you seem to find a special delight in missing it; you often resemble the stubborn ox or the braying ass. You do make funny noises, and invent amusing philosophies; you are endlessly inventive (like father, like son) — perhaps one day you will grow up, perhaps one day you will invent only good. I have sustained you as I sustained your ancestors. They, too, were not very bright — but remarkably entertaining. I have been with you since the beginning of time, for time itself began with me. I have often waited in vain for you to speak to me; I've been right here beside you, through all your virtues and all your crimes. You can't drive me away. You often imagine I've deserted you; you often imagine I do not exist. The trouble is, you do not often think; you are more easily and more quickly discouraged than any other creature I have made. Quite regularly, you ignore me — except in great distress; you love me mightily when you think you need me, and forget me altogether when I supply your need. You're an odd-ball and a bird brain, but I love you. I have never forsaken you. I knew your father and his father. One day I shall know your children's children. They will know more than you do, but there will still be plenty left to know.

"No matter where you go, you'll find me — on the moon, in holy Russia, or in holy (or heathen?) America. I am the outer, and the inner, universe; outside me, there's no place to go.

"You sometimes imagine that I'm interested only in religion, but I never heard the word till you invented it. Wherever you meet Love, the Joy of the World, the Sweet Mystery of Life, you meet me. Wherever you meet Power — all the power there is in planets and persons — you meet me. Wherever you meet Faithfulness — the faithfulness that sustains, heals, and advances the total life of nature and man — you meet me. Wherever you meet Fruitfulness — in sex or in soul — you meet me. Wherever you meet Fellowship — the goal of all human endeavor, and the way — you meet me; for I am the life in all that lives, the power to exist and move in all that exists and moves. There is only one of me, yet you meet me in your mirror; you encounter me on land, on sea, and in the air — in outer and inner space. Not all your teachings about me are true, but I am used to being misrepresented (especially by my friends). I knew you before you were born; I will gather you to my bosom when you die, and I shall cherish your memory in my heart always.

"You haven't evolved very far, but you are, after all, on the way. Rome wasn't built in a day, and it is doubtful if it was worth building. I cannot, and I do not, expect too much too fast. I remember the frailty of your frame; I recall that you are talking dust. The false things you build collapse of their own weight. Whatever makes you empty, superficial, shallow, is my enemy because it is your enemy; it has no final hope of success. Whatever makes you your neighbor's enemy makes you also your own, from the rising to the going down of the sun. Whatever exalts class or caste or creed or color above community is my enemy, because it is your enemy; it cannot last; it has no permanence, no staying power in its contest with me. If I removed these things too rapidly, I would remove you also, for these things proceed from you. I am the Good Physician, and my operating knife is history — life itself. The surgery is well under way, and its speed has greatly increased. I shall separate the darkness from the light in your mind, in your institutions. I am the Lord; my presence is the heavens and the earth; beside me there is no other; outside me there is nothing at all. You are in my hand, and I will see you through.

"You are very serious, very solemn; you forget that the Lord loves a merry heart; that your face is long is evidence enough that your faith is short. Sometimes in a flash you see the point — that I am your life and the life of all — and a smile breaks out upon your soul; your heart sings with thanksgiving, and you know that the distant God is also near — without beginning and without end."

BOOK THREE

TOWARD "COMMUNITY MAN"

Thinking forward to the growth of his word in their minds, Jesus said to his disciples: " No longer do I call you servants . . . ; but I have called you friends " (John 15:15, RSV) — not subordinates but individuals, younger brothers, co-workers for the practical growth of love in human life. He taught them to pray, " Thy will be done, on earth " (Matt. 6:10, RSV).

Community — whether here or there or everywhere — is the creation of the Holy Spirit. It is therefore never static or stagnant, wholly unlike its ersatz substitute, collectivism. On the contrary, it unites the new with the old; it is always dynamic. And it is so because — always in principle and increasingly in practice — it stimulates, encourages, provides for, and protects the needed social criticism of nonconformist personalities and minorities. Its first law is the right to disagree, the right to be different, together with the right to unbroken fellowship, the right to mutual respect and acceptance.

Community constitutes an open, as against a closed, mind, an open, as against a closed, society; creative fellowship across real difference, the charity of the Spirit, is its constant goal and its growing achievement. Not uniformity but communion is its motif. It seeks not the cancellation but the enrichment of variety.

To community man, all men are, and are learning to be, one family, on one planet, in one universe; the objective is one world across all kinds of " local color," and the growth of individuals big enough in mind and heart to sustain and enrich it. Our churches of all faiths sometimes lead the retreat to collectivism, but more often nurture selfhood and serve as trail guides to community. At their best, they are channels of creative energy, agents of the Holy Spirit.

To community man, a real dialogue, a true dialectic, a growing communion, is both probable and essential between men of all races, classes, cultures, and ideologies; further, the freedom that makes brotherhood possible, and the brotherhood that makes freedom necessary, are seen to form the substance and character of all democracy worth preserving and improving.

10

The Right to Personal Privacy

A natural question immediately arises: "Where and how does community begin? Does it start outside or inside the individual?" Undoubtedly it can be externally encouraged and protected by custom and constitution; it is the business of government, of all government, to provide this encouragement and protection — or prepare for revolution! Community can be, and must be, externally supported; it cannot be externally guaranteed; in essence, it is self-transcendence which begins with self-acceptance; it is therefore *personal privacy* in mind and heart — God's sanctuary in the soul. You might call it freedom of speech, of thought, of conscience, and of faith — the freedom of the Spirit. If community does not start with selfhood and self-acceptance, it does not start!

The greatest sin of parents against their growing children is the habit of always and forever making up their minds for them, riding roughshod over their personal privacy, ignoring or shouting down their personal convictions, refusing to allow them the right to think and act on the basis of inner integrity — the privilege parents usually insist upon for themselves. How shall an adolescent learn to accept responsibility for his ideas if he is never permitted to form them, or, having formed them, is never permitted to carry them out? The greatest need of any individual, whether adolescent or adult, is self-respect — the right to speak, to think, and to act in accordance with his own present understanding; without it, no community is possible; without it, none is desirable! When you take away self-respect from anyone, whether young or old, all you have left is a parasite — a man full-grown in body but infantile in mind, waiting helplessly for someone to tell him, under any and all conditions, what to think and what to do — a caricature, not a character. It is less serious to rob a human being of his money than of his self-respect, his personal right to be wrong, if need be, and to learn from being wrong. Money can be replaced, but a withered self-respect may never grow again!

It is hard, very hard, for a parent to acquire the skill, the patience, the forbearance, to stand aside, especially in words, and allow a growing adolescent to make his own mistakes, to use or misuse his personal privacy of mind and heart, the gift of the Spirit. We parents are quick to resent contradiction and correction by our children, both in public and in private; we are sometimes slow to restrain our own habit of contradicting and correcting our children. Parents deserve real sympathy in this regard, for no one easily develops the ability to let other individuals think and act in accordance with their own convictions.

However, community means responsibility: parents are responsible for their children's behavior, their children's instruction. No true parent will stand aside, with piously folded hands, while his child involves himself in ideas and deeds that may cripple or destroy him. Parents also have the right to speak, to think, and to act in accordance with conscience and faith. Their self-respect is a community right too. Like anybody else, they are entitled to be *heard*.

Nonetheless, adolescents deserve real sympathy too. There is an invisible line, eternally drawn, between the parental right to express an honest opinion, and something different in kind — parental dictatorship which robs the child of self-respect. Advice, when it is needed and asked for, is always in order — provided it is not accompanied with threats, either spoken or implied. In simplest terms, if a parent wishes to be listened to with respect, he must acquire the difficult skill of listening with respect to his child. If he wishes to be accepted, he must also accept — and this is the character of community, the creation of the Spirit of Christ. There is more than meets the eye in the words, " Do unto others — your children, for example — as you would have them do unto you " (Matt. 7:12, RSV, paraphrase).

The hardest job in the world for any parent is to restrain himself, to deny himself, to hold himself back — and thus deeply and genuinely to grant his growing child personal honesty of mind and heart, the grace of the Spirit. It is the hardest thing to do; it is also the most necessary and vital. Further, it is the greatest gift any parent can give his child — the gift of self-respect, of self-responsibility, of membership in the community. Without this gift, patiently and genuinely given, the normal adolescent, sooner or later, will revolt. The parent would revolt quickly enough if someone dictated to him on any and all occasions.

To give our children the uninvaded privacy of personal conviction that we demand for ourselves — this, I believe, is the first law of healthy and stimulating partnership, of community, in parent-child relations. One Holy Spirit is the architect of community — and the Father of freedom.

The first law of happy husband-wife relations, of partnership or community in marriage, is exactly the same. A husband who does not grant his wife the right of personal privacy, of independent thought and action, will accumulate for himself much sorrow. Having sown the wind, he will reap the whirlwind. Naturally, he will then blame all his sorrow on his wife.

The popular view may be correct — that husbands are the traditional offenders in this regard, possibly because society has given them, or they have taken, and taken too seriously, the notion that the man is head of the house. On the other hand, the notion that the husband is head of the house may be a myth, a device of self-protection invented by men to help them balance the unequal budget of power, a secret acknowledgment that actual power has always been the private prerogative of wives. In any case, I am convinced that unhappiness in wives is often caused by husbands with dictator complexes. Whether it is the husband or the wife who refuses to grant the other the right of personal privacy, the right of community, the refusal itself, it seems to me, is the primary source of all marital discord, the major single cause of divorce. Wives who give in habitually to dictatorial husbands usually develop nervous breakdowns, or the mentality of slaves; they become fearful of the sound of their own voices, afraid to have an opinion on anything, quick to abandon every independent idea that occurs to them. They are objects of pity — glassy-eyed nincompoops, with vacant, frightened faces. Now and then, with all self-respect denied, a wife can stand her enforced claustrophobia no longer — and strikes a blow for freedom. Which simply means that dictatorship, in any form, produces either infantilism or open rebellion. The second enemy of slavery is the human spirit; slavery's first enemy is the Holy Spirit.

One must try to be fair about this thing, for husbands are not always the offenders. Sometimes wives let themselves go, perhaps to compensate for their own childhood when parents denied them all personal privacy; they then become self-appointed army top sergeants; they make a full-time career out of telling the one lone " buck private," the husband committed to their charge, what to think, say, and do under any and all conditions. The husband then becomes either a grown infantile, a glassy-eyed nincompoop, with vacant stare, or launches a revolt of his own in search of self-respect. Who but the Holy Spirit reduces the mouse in the man?

A similar rebellion develops when teachers deny their students the right of personal privacy, freedom of thought and action — the foundation of community. The teacher who dictates the answers, who fails to practice self-restaint, produces student conformists and yes men, whose self-respect has withered — or students in revolt, who regurgitate in final exams what the teacher has forced down their throats, but assimilate none of it.

The original American idea, both politically and religiously, was the same: every human, whether we like him or not, is a child of God, with an inner life, the creation of the Spirit — whether or not he has been allowed to develop selfhood, and whether or not we are capable of recognizing it. As a child of God, every human has, and is entitled to preserve, a magic circle of selfhood which God himself does not invade. We learn through experience — that is, through trial and error — but we learn nothing unless the experience, with all its trial and error, is in some degree self-initiated, is actually our own. When we are denied individual selfhood, personal privacy, we either submit weakly and become slaves — or revolt and strike a blow for freedom. What else were the American colonists doing when they held their famous Boston Tea Party, and dumped His Majesty's property into the sea — refusing to be treated like something less than men, something less than equals, with equal rights? The American Revolution was produced, not by half-baked hotheads, as is sometimes thought, but simply by men who refused to be denied the God-given right of community — of self-respect and self-initiative. The deadliest enemy of the enemies of freedom is *Agapē,* the Spirit of Christ.

When Europeans decided to stand up to Hitler and his henchmen, they regained their essential humanity, their heroism, their self-respect, long plowed under by nazi tyranny. The Holy Spirit similarly replaced the Christians' fear with faith before the Roman legions! The martyrs knew nothing of conformist cowardice before Nero, Hadrian, and Diocletian!

Today, it seems, and not alone in Russia, men have grown used to being pushed around by their governments; independence of thought and action appears to be dead; men seem neither to value it nor desire it; mediocrity and conformity appear to hold undisputed sway. It is not quite true, but often seems true, that when we want to know what to think, we write our Congressman; when an idea occurs to us, we inquire of the FBI whether we are permitted to hold it; we set aside all creative originality till we have cleared it with the House Committee on Un-American Activities.

These appearances, however, are deceiving. Underneath our superficial capitulation to current majority opinion, we are, in fact, still human. The demand for personal privacy, for community, is a built-in feature of human character. "It is God that hath made us, and not we ourselves." (Ps. 100:3, KJV.) We may be on our way to the mentality of slaves, to collectivism, to the glassy-eyed, vacant stare of nincompoops. Fortunately, there is no guarantee that we will continue that way. One day — history is full of examples — the Holy Spirit may reignite our human spirits; the demand for selfhood and self-respect may again be heard — as in Hungary. At any moment we may weary of claustrophobia, in politics and in religion, and strike a blow for freedom.

There is, of course, no easy road, no simple short cut, to community, to emotional and rational maturity, to self-respect and self-transcendence, whether we are parents or children, married or single, teachers or students, politicians or people. Maturity of any kind is achieved only through struggle and reflection — the anguish of life, and the anguish of thought. Clearly, it can be achieved more easily if its character is understood. Community is the poise and peace of *Agapē,* the Spirit's presence and power; it is selfhood and the will to preserve selfhood in others, the ability to think our own thoughts and live by them, yet to stand aside, and let other people act as their inner integrity demands.

To barge into another man's home is the crime called housebreaking. To barge into another man's mind, to push our way into another man's privacy, to thrust our opinions down another man's throat — this is the father of all crimes. As Paul put it: " Who are you to pass judgment on the servant of another? It is before his own master that he stands or falls. . . . God has welcomed him." (Rom. 14:3, 4, RSV.)

Where your freedom of speech, of thought, of conscience, and of faith begins — there my right to interfere ends — whether you are my wife, my husband, my child, my parent, my student, my teacher, or my congressman. We must draw " the magic line," " the community line," between us — not because we don't love one another, but because we do. We are called to be our brother's helper, not his hangman — his ally, neither a nuisance, a ring in his nose, nor a noose around his neck. One thing everyone wants is help, guidance, but only when he is ready to receive it. At times we all need mothering; no one, any time, needs smothering. It is just the Holy Spirit, moving in our human spirits, that creates our

fellowship and quickens our faithfulness, yet protects and preserves our freedom. In the words of Paul: "For freedom Christ
has set us free; stand fast therefore, and do not submit again to a
yoke of slavery." (Gal. 5:1, RSV.)

11

The Right to Fellowship Across Difference

The most difficult lesson we humans, so recently emerged from
the Stone Age, have to learn is this: the right of every man to full
respect and full fellowship across honest difference of conviction.
You might put it this way: the right to disagree is the meaning of
dignity; however painful, it is good, it is creative, that we do not
all think alike. Conversely, the right to fellowship, real fellowship,
across honest disagreement, is the meaning of community, the demand and gift of the Holy Spirit. No matter how loudly we shout
"Democracy," it does not exist, not anywhere at all, except where
men have acquired the emotional maturity, the intellectual de-
tachment, to respect and love one another, as close friends, across
the widest possible chasms of divergent conclusion. Do we have
to agree, about politics, about science, about religion, or about anything, to be friends? If we do, we have, not community, not democracy, but nationalism, imperialism, fanaticism. If on the other
hand, we can work and walk together, across vital disagreement,
spiritual community is already here.

In America, the "right to fellowship across honest disagreement" was not first developed in education or religion. The Bill
of Rights was primarily a secular achievement, though its meaning is the essence of creative religion. The founding fathers, so
recently escaped from political persecution by assorted religious
orthodoxies in Europe, were determined to write into the charter
of this nation the first principle of spiritual community — respect

for difference of conviction — to make impossible the hounding of nonconformists as subversives. Often enough, to be sure, they forgot the principle in practice, as we do in our treatment of minorities, yet, generally speaking, the American record is as good as any and probably better than most. On these shores, for example, Catholics and Protestants may not persecute each other — officially. When you remember that the right to disagree, without penalty, was achieved in Czechoslovakia in 1920 through the intervention of Woodrow Wilson (and that right is now already lost), you can see that the American freedom to differ, achieved in the eighteenth century, was not behind the rest of the world. Today we may or may not be " 'way behind " Russia in the mastery of " outer " space; if reports are correct about Russia's propensity to kill all her nonconformists, she is " 'way behind " us in the mastery of " inner " space, the freedom of the Spirit. We may be another Athens — struggling for intellectual or spiritual liberty against another Sparta!

Our recurrent difficulty is this: the right to fellowship across disagreement, a primary spiritual right, was written into our secular government, primarily for protection against religious fanaticism; political and racial fanaticism then seemed of less immediate concern. However, constructive tolerance in every area is the clear meaning of the words: " All men are created equal." Our American two-party system preserves the right to disagree — up to a point — in politics. One may even be an Independent without loss of life or limb. Nonetheless, we have still a considerable way to go to achieve, in practice and in law, the right to fellowship across difference — in other conflicts. For example, the right of racial and religious minorities to exist, on terms of equal justice, alongside majorities — without excommunication from schools or churches or government jobs — is a further extension of the right to fellowship, a primary human right, a God-given human right, that we are only beginning to understand. The root of the problem of the Jew — in the Middle East or the Middle West — is this: the way of the transgressor is hard, whether the trangression is racial, creedal, or economic. Just as we do, the

Jew insists, in faith and in life, on the right to be different, the right to be what he is and to believe what he must. Also as we do, he longs secretly to be fully recognized, fully accepted as a legitimate member of the human race, a respected member of the fraternity of God, with all the legal and moral privileges thereto pertaining. Segregation in the United States, like "apartheid" in South Africa, is evidence enough that creative tolerance (the right to fellowship across difference) is, as yet, more principle than practice — everywhere. Further, our recent hysterical lust for thought control indicates how far we have yet to go to apply, in our minds and in our institutions, the right to fellowship across difference which the founding fathers voyaged a long hard way to establish.

On any showing, there is something in us all (it is sometimes called "original sin") that resists the granting of the right to fellowship to every man and all men. Perhaps the trouble is our natural instinct for self-preservation. The existence of views other than our own, particularly on subjects of depth concern, constitutes, we feel, a threat to our survival. Perhaps simple intellectual laziness is the root of the difficulty. Other beliefs than ours disturb our self-approval. Rather than weigh the alternatives as dispassionately as we can, and perhaps grow a little, we take the easy way out and attempt to exterminate both the disagreement and the movements or persons who disagree — by law if we can, by mob action if we cannot. Exactly in this way, a Christ was crucified! It was precisely his crucifixion that made us aware of the source of sorrow!

What little actual civilization we have thus far achieved, it seems, hangs by a hair. Even its continuance, at the present level, cannot be taken for granted. Creative tolerance is hard to come by, and, once understood, hard to live by. Yet its growth is synonymous with the growth of civilization. That we are, at present, not more than half civilized is self-evident. There is still in us, too near the surface, an unholy delight in barbecuing heretics! With what wholehearted devotion we shout for "our team" at a football game — or for our race or creed against all outsiders —

in the market place, and the Assembly of the United Nations! We orthodox theologians, sometimes quick to create crusades against dissenting minorities, should be able to recognize that our passion to exterminate disagreement constitutes, in itself, a convincing evidence of partial human depravity — to begin with, our own!

The fact that creative tolerance is difficult to live by in no way exempts us from the necessity of learning to live by it. The lust for conformity, like any other disease, is curable. We have made some headway against polio, once called incurable; there is evidence that we may, in the near future, make real headway against so-called incurable cancer. To consider any disease incurable before you begin is to get nowhere in curing it. A moral disease, like the lust for conformity, is probably no more difficult than polio or cancer to bring under control. With all the darkness that is in us (we are, after all, the grandchildren of cave men), there is also in us, in every one of us, an actual depth longing for fellowship, for spiritual or human community — for our children and their children, but also for ourselves. We are beginning to understand — more than superficially — that we cannot preserve the right to fellowship across difference for ourselves, unless we defend it also — in law and practice — for all races, classes, and creeds. We are beginning to see that it is hard to achieve community, but much harder not to! The alternative is extinction!

All orthodoxies, whether scientific, political, or religious, face a perpetual predicament. Our greatest human need is growth, in science, in government, in relevant religion — above all, in creative tolerance, the foundation of community and dignity, the disturbing demand of the Holy Spirit. Orthodoxy, which considers its partial truth total, final, and infallible, makes growth impossible. What sin against humanity and against God is more unpardonable than to believe our present knowledge, in science, in religion, or in government, beyond improvement? Precisely this sin, the assumption of present adequacy, beheaded Paul, burned John Hus and Servetus at the stake, drove the Pilgrims aboard the *Mayflower* to seek in a new world the right to think *ahead*. In other words, all orthodoxy, allergic to criticism, allergic to growth, allergic to fellowship across difference, allergic to freedom, is itself *unorthodox!*

Orthodoxies, of all varieties, do about as much harm as they do good. It is true that they provide a necessary continuity in human relations; they help to maintain order and sanity — while men seek the better and the more. Tradition, another word for orthodoxy, is, after all, the memory of mankind. The past has taught us something. Amnesia, whether racial or personal, is a doubtful asset. The trouble with orthodoxy is its ambiguity: on the one hand it gives us a scientific, political, or religious faith; it preserves a sense of community with our fathers and our children; on the other hand, it sometimes makes us frenzied fanatics, ready, at any moment, to sacrifice the lives and limbs of men (as honest as ourselves!) who dare to disagree.

For what other reason have we, throughout history, " excommunicated " from our fellowship the creative minorities and creative personalities from whom all growth has come? The way of the critic, the nonconformist, the incarnate social conscience, is as hard as the way of the transgressor — and *for the same reason.* As Dostoevsky pointed out: God keeps seven righteous men, seven clear-eyed critics, alive in every generation — and with them weaves a new world!

When all is said and done, integrity is more productive than authority. According to Thomas Hobbes, the word " heresy " was first used in ancient Greece, where it meant simply " having an opinion " — any kind of opinion, in agreement or disagreement with authority; only a ruler was entitled to " have an opinion "! Honesty of mind has made men heretics — a name applied to them by one or another orthodoxy — but a heretic, after all, is merely a man who sees an important truth not included in the presently popular formula. Should we succeed in exterminating our heretics, including Russia, the current heretic of the nations, all growth toward community and dignity might be ended; our glory might be one with Nineveh and Tyre. As Reinhold Niebuhr has said:

" A tragic and revealing aspect of the experience of the Christian ages is that, again and again, ' publicans and sinners ' have had to rescue an important aspect of truth about life, and restore wholesomeness into human relations, against the fanaticism of Christian saints, who had forgotten that sainthood is corrupted whenever holiness is claimed as a simple possession."

Disagreement, when it issues from long study and honest struggle to get to the root of a problem, is more duty than delight. With considerable reluctance, Amos, Hosea, Micah, Isaiah, and Jeremiah accepted this duty — for the sake of community; to them it proved more pain than privilege; we cherish with words, but seldom emulate with deeds, their example. As Jesus in effect put it: " We murder God's prophets, then pray at their tombs! "

The word " Christianity " means many things to many men: to some it means an infallible creed, a magic ritual, a defensive fragment (a spore) firmly closed against fellowship with all mankind! To others it means that all men everywhere are accepted, sustained, comforted, and justified by universal personal grace, yet everlastingly called by the same grace to growth in the practice of love. We can do nothing against the truth! If Christianity, on any definition, is true, it has nothing to lose — it has everything to gain — by listening, as well as preaching, to its critics and competitors; as the European theologian Hendrik Kraemer has emphasized, Christianity loses its own soul, its own *Agapē* character, when it refuses to grant to all men and every man the same freedom of thought and expression it demands for itself. An ethical world community is on its way to us from the future, because God, who *is* God, is *one* God; that his will (always other than and better than our understanding of it) be done on earth is more important, and more necessary, than that it be called " Christian." We ourselves are more interested in contents than in labels! Can God be less intelligent than we?

The word " capitalism " likewise means many things to many men: to some it means the right of the strong to fleece the weak; to others, it means the right of the weak to organize, to resist being fleeced, to achieve better work and better income. If capitalism, however defined, is true, it has nothing to lose — it has much to gain — by listening to, as well as decrying, its critics and competitors; it loses its own soul, its own character, when it refuses to grant to every honest viewpoint the same "free enterprise" in thought and action that it demands for itself.

Creative tolerance, it should be clear, is a wholly different thing from "having no opinion." An empty mind is no doubt an "open" mind, though vacant houses are usually "closed" and "locked"; the empty mind is easygoing, because it is going nowhere; it requires "no stoop, no squat, no squint" — but also represents no struggle, no effort, no risk, no venture; it makes a perfect score, "no runs, no hits, no errors." It is refreshing in children, and in childlike folk, after too long an association with dogmatists, whether political, scientific, or religious. Creative tolerance lives in a different street altogether! It characterizes the mind, at one and the same time, both closed and open. Closed because it has struggled to see something, believes that it does see it, and is determined that its truth be heard and weighed in the councils of men. Without this kind of mind, there would be no heretics, no critics, no conscience — and consequently no growth in our knowledge and brotherhood; a heretic is usually a man who thinks deeply, so deeply, in fact, that he is willing to be burned at the stake rather than surrender the truth he sees, a truth as yet not widely accepted. Integrity is not another word for vacuity; it is another word for anguish and insight. As a rule, the men who really respect other people's views are also the men who really respect their own — realizing the holy precariousness, the margin for error, which must, and does, accompany the truest thinking of man.

In other words, God is near! Therefore, believe (without cowardice) what you believe, or you can neither live by it nor learn its true value nor sell it. At the same time, doubt, test, and question what you believe, or it won't be worth selling. As Paul put it: "Prove [or test] all things; hold fast that which is good." (I Thess. 5:21, KJV.) The creative mind is always open as well as closed; it is willing to listen (respectfully, sympathetically, intelligently) to divergent views, as it rightly demands that its own be listened to; it knows that its truth, even the truth it has suffered to see, and God's truth are not, and cannot be, exactly identical. There are more things in heaven and in earth than are, as yet, included in any science, religion, or political philosophy.

The one fold with one shepherd, on its way to us, will transcend, include, housebreak, and domesticate most of our present divisions, scientific, political, and religious; it will be characterized not by uniformity but by variety, an infinitely greater variety than we have as yet conceived; the dead hand of infallibility (of standardized and sanctified boredom, of organized "hohum") will be replaced by the living hand of fellowship across wide and colorful difference.

As Luther insisted, no man has the right to claim or assume lordship over another's mind — in politics, in education, or in religion. Often enough, to be sure, Paul was not overly tolerant; after all, he was riding herd on high-spirited yearlings. He once wrote to his young disciple Timothy: "Charge some that they teach no other doctrine. . . . If any man teach otherwise . . . he is proud, knowing nothing." (I Tim. 1:3; 6:3, 4, KJV.) Fortunately for us, James, Peter, and John taught differently, and their words too are included, and valued, in our New Testament. But Paul, like the rest of us, had his better moments. On another occasion he said that charity is more to the point than either creed or crusade; he also said, " Not that we lord it over your faith; we work with you for your joy " (II Cor. 1:24, RSV). To heal, to help, is a duty, a demand; to dictate, to dominate, is to suffocate and destroy.

Faith is honest conviction, and honest conviction turns the motors of all forward movement. Hope is productive; it sees what is not yet here, and marches forth with bands and banners to welcome it. Greater than either is Love, which builds and heals the whole life of man, for Love is creative tolerance, the presence and sweetness of the Holy Spirit. Everyone knows the law of the jungle; real fellowship across real difference is the law of the clearing — the earthly community of " God with men."

12

Fellowship Is the Goal and the Way
— in Knowledge

All that we like to call knowledge is, as a matter of fact, fifty-one (or ninety?) per cent ignorance, yet the percentage, on any showing, is reducible! For this reason, schools, colleges, and churches exist, and nothing is one hundred per cent effective, not even death and taxes. All that is called knowledge is our human attempt to understand what we experience, whether a faraway thing like the United Nations, or a thing near at hand like the universe. If we realize that our conclusions are more or less superficial, that our opinions (even our best opinions) are not infallible, there is always some value — some *real* value — in the attempt.

Responsible, as against irresponsible knowledge, issues from honest and sustained struggle to probe beneath the surface of a problem. Truth that will hold up under all kinds of tests (*inviolate* truth) is worth pursuing with complete concern! Exact and total truth no doubt is beyond our present grasp, perhaps beyond our human grasp, in science as in religion. But we never know till we try — and not always then! Socrates found that the " wise " men of his time were not only ignorant, but ignorant of the fact that they were ignorant; if he had any claim to wisdom, it lay in his awareness that all human knowledge is limited. A productive awareness of one's own ignorance, it is clear, accompanies advanced knowledge. Pride is more common among the uninformed. Humility usually marks the pioneer who has pressed farther ahead than the rest of us. A better understanding of the real,

the true, and the sane, has set him free from two silly stupidities
— *relativism* on the one hand (the philosophy of bird brains),
and *dogmatism* on the other (the *rigor mortis* of the mind).

On one occasion I spent an hour with an allergy specialist, a
competent M.D. He asked me many questions, but produced no
hypodermic needle. I said, " Aren't you going to puncture my
arm sixty times — as before? " He replied, " We don't use that
method any more; we found that it was never more than fifteen
per cent reliable." When you stop to think about it, the American people spent ten million dollars, or more, on the procedure
now discarded. They were not deliberately robbed — just robbed;
the best method then available was used — though later pro-
nounced useless. The doctor explained, " You will have to watch
yourself." I already knew that, of course. I asked, " Isn't there
some kind of injection that will neutralize my worst hay fever
attacks? " " Yes," he said. " We have developed forty-two specific
antihistamines. All you have to do is try one each time a food
allergy gets you down; we will then know which is effective." I
am afflicted with allergy fever about once a year; to try a specific
neutralizer at each attack would require forty-two years. I would
then need not a doctor but an undertaker. As I left, I said, " I am
a doctor of philosophy, and you are a doctor of medicine, but isn't
it the simple truth that there is no such thing as adequate knowledge on any subject under the sun? " He agreed; we shook hands;
he never sent me a bill.

The story may represent, more accurately than you think, the
present state of all human knowledge. I am not complaining; I
shall continue to trust the doctor, who does his best to apply the
findings of centuries of research. Responsible knowledge, though
less than adequate, has paid the price of long struggle to draw
near the relevant truth, to separate knowledge from superstition.
Without the effort to know what is really true, we would be nowhere at all.

No knowledge, now in hand, is absolute; yet all knowledge is
about the Absolute. No man knows the universe fully; all men
know the universe — limitedly. As Paul insisted, " We know *in*

part." All the time we are dealing with reality, with God; all the time reality, or God, is dealing with us; some actual light shines in our minds — through, and in spite of, our best truth and our worst error.

The man in the street, and the world-weary college sophomore, conclude (with a shrug of their shoulders, and with the Preacher of old) that the pursuit of better knowledge is a striving after wind. Without the constant pursuit of truer truth (so to speak), not by somebody here and there but by everybody everywhere, we return automatically to the Stone Age, the altars of human sacrifice, and primeval gloom. The striking thing is not that we have made so little progress in knowledge across the centuries, but that we have made any. In appearance, at least, some real progress is discernible; the discovery of the moral law by Moses and Jesus was both an advance over, and a break with, the lawless tyranny and slavery of Pharaoh and Caesar. The honest thinking of Abraham, Buddha, Socrates, and Luther was, and remains, clear gain — compared with the mythologies and idolatries of Ur, Benares, Athens, and Rome. We no longer throw unwanted infants into nearby sewers, as the Romans did; we no longer consider that the sick are demon possessed, or afflicted by God and not to be helped or healed for fear of his wrath. Mental and physical slavery, in part, is still a sociological and spiritual fact, yet we no longer take it for granted or give it our unqualified consent. Caste systems prevail on every continent, including our own, yet the Holy Spirit, the idea of brotherhood, of community, if not the full practice, is abroad, and gaining ground.

What little knowledge we can be said to have, it is clear, is the fruit of long, slow, painful effort (the heroism of the Spirit) against all kinds of intellectual, social, and spiritual resistance. It is a cumulative achievement of community-in-humanity, the image of community-in-Deity (our basic Trinitarian faith). Individuals have played the part of pioneers, usually against majority opinion, yet sooner or later the truths discerned by the few have become the distorted but accepted orthodoxy of the many. The story of science, as James B. Conant and J. W. N. Sullivan have presented it, is a long demonstration of increased knowledge through individual failure and community success — or vice versa. No scientist stands only on his own feet; he stands also on the shoulders of sturdy trail blazers. Social science is not as new as it imagines; Confucius had no other concern than the rational reduction of community conflict. Government, philosophy, economics, and religion are diverse demonstrations of one struggle to know, one determination to find and walk in the light — by creative centuries, whole generations, and lonely individuals. *All knowledge, whether half or whole, is the product of fellowship, the teamwork of the Holy Spirit.*

The knowledge now in our possession, in science, philosophy, and religion, is not only the child of community — but its parent as well; that is, it exists for no other reason than to increase fellowship, in depth and breadth, in every area of life. Both science and religion, at times, have been nationalized and thus prostituted to the self-interest of ruling states, Nordic races, and " infallible " creeds (of the Left and of the Right), yet in themselves science and religion recognize no national or racial or creedal boundaries. Both are transnational, transracial, and transcreedal.

Complete concern for the common good means that knowledge (though an end as a means) is never an end in itself; all knowledge exists to be sought by persistent and dedicated men, yet also and only for the increase of dignity and community, not to enslave man but to set him free. The present front of knowledge is everywhere; there is work enough to go around (help yourself!). Desperate is our need for better knowledge in psychic and physical healing; without better knowledge in government, economics, and social change, life itself can be destroyed in our time. An increase of relevance in religion is not a secondary matter, for religion is the quality of all our endeavor. As Julian Huxley has pointed out, we have only begun to grasp the potential atomic energy (so to speak) of the mind:

" It is perfectly possible that today man's so-called supernormal or extrasensory faculties are in the same case as were his mathematical faculties during the first or second glaciation of the Ice Age — barely

more than a potentiality, with no technique for eliciting and develop-
ing them, no tradition behind them to give them continuity and intellectual respectability. Even such simple performances as multiplying
two three-figure numbers would have appeared entirely magical to
early Stone Age men. . . .

"Some people at least possess possibilities of knowledge which are
not confined within the ordinary channels of sense-perception. . . . If
we could discover in what this faculty really consists, on what mech-
anism it depends, and by what conditions and agencies it can be influenced, it should be capable of development like any other human faculty. Man may thus be unique in more ways than he now suspects."

Undoubtedly our greatest immediate need is better knowledge
in international and interpersonal relations — the "traffic snarl"
of modern life, our troubled attempt to think and act together,
across all our differences, on one shrinking (and shrieking)
planet. Without growth in this kind of knowledge, our earth
could become, even more than it is, "the insane asylum of the
universe." I think it is, in fact, a cradle or a nursery. Jesus understood the urgency of our need; he said: "Would that even today you knew the things that make for peace! But now they are
hid from your eyes" (Luke 19:42, RSV). We possess infinite
know-how and can-do in war production, but feeble and finite
competence in peace production. Peace production requires mature skills beyond any we have yet developed; unlike Paul, who
put away childish things as he came to adult years, we have put
away the wisdom of maturity and returned to the immaturity
(the folly, the organized imbecility) of war. Gadgets excite us;
good will bores us. We yearn for bigger bombs and bigger rock-
ets; we yawn at better knowledge, better wisdom, better men.
Adult (as counted in centuries), we continue to think and act
like citizens of the Stone Age (our racial childhood). How to
achieve and maintain community in humanity — this knowledge
is a central necessity, a necessity for survival; it is not a peripheral
luxury.

Nothing in the nature of things prevents a basic shift in our
present preoccupation with war gadgets to better knowledge of
human relations. Nothing in "science" requires that its attention

be devoted (solely) to "mechanics." At any moment scientists of the spirit (we used to call them "saints") may appear, indeed have already appeared, among us! In so far as the word "science" has come to mean, in the popular mind, only the tiresome production of pills and power machines, it has lost its soul, its breadth and depth of character, and is now rationally bankrupt. Better knowledge in human relations, on the wide scale of world community, was always, and is now, the "queen" of the sciences. The fact that a few "scientists" are turning their careful research in this direction is the hope of tomorrow. Everyone has heard of Kinsey's elaborate studies of sexual behavior — the basis of physical survival; not so many have heard of Sorokin's even more elaborate studies of altruistic (or responsible or moral) behavior — the basis alike of human survival and of human evolution.

No one can know, or do, everything, to be sure; division of labor, specialization, is a necessity in the community pursuit of better knowledge. Science, government, economics, and religion are, and will remain, independent pursuits; their effective contribution depends on their freedom, their autonomy; yet they are not activities in separate worlds; they are not even, of necessity, the activities of separate men; all inhabit one world; all are the struggles of man as man to achieve community and dignity. Science, thought, and faith are not three concerns, but three forms of one concern, one thrust of the Holy Spirit; they are three activities of one human mind, within and for one human family. No division of labor, no specialization, is self-sufficient. All individual and community effort to achieve better knowledge constitutes one human endeavor to separate sense from nonsense, that sense may prevail and heal the whole of human life. Knowledge has come a long way; it has a longer way to go. We are, after all, but recently, or partially, emancipated aborigines.

The fear of Federal aid to college education is the fear of intellectual regimentation and moral mediocrity — the present status, more or less, of our tax-supported primary and secondary schools. This fear is justified. Yet education has always been, will always remain, a community responsibility. Any aid to education that does not encroach upon the freedom of the mind is better than none. If education, when aided by government, ceases to pursue inviolate truth with complete concern, whose fault is it? It is not really the fault of government. It is the fault, not of the aid, but of the aided.

The fear that secular education will strangle religion is ambiguous; secular education, it is true, does tend to lose depth and breadth, to leave the student misinformed or uninformed about every aspect of human experience, including religion — both as a subject in its own right and as the moral or rational quality of every subject. More deeply, the fear has no justification, for the purpose of education is to educate; all education worthy of the name is, at one and the same time, both quantitative and qualitative, both secular and religious. Even secular students need to know, are entitled to know, as much about Moses, Buddha, and Jesus as about Alexander, Napoleon, and Hitler. Only one fear is justified — that all education, whether public or private, will be poor, feeble, and futile.

We are beginning to understand better than formerly that adults, on the average, need education, of a qualitative as well as quantitative kind, as much as or more than children do. Adult education is the unexplored continent in our time. What little exists is largely of trade school quality — good in itself, but not enough. Some of us are determined to do something about it; we have set up personally conducted " liberal arts " reading courses, primarily for individuals but also for discussion groups. Seven of these courses (each at minimum cost, each designed to provide fifteen minutes of daily reading for a full year) are now available to anyone, anywhere, young or old, who desires keenly to kick over the mental motors a bit, to push back the spiritual frontiers, to stay young. Travel, for example, if only with a book by the fireside, can mean the discovery of men and ideas across centuries as well as across continents and communions.

Our education, at present, is one-sided, incomplete, and adolescent — on all levels, undergraduate and graduate alike. When modern men become aware of the breadth and depth of their present ignorance on all subjects, will they not develop an intellectual curiosity, an appetite for knowledge, beyond anything we have yet seen? I think so. Even the Sputnik may prove a blessing in disguise; from any point of view, it is a stimulant — to thought, to a better mastery of " inner " space!

Human fellowship (the presence and product of the Holy Spirit) begins in deeds, and not in " words only," when one person alone, or two or three together as Jesus said, start reading and thinking universally, probing to the root of things, with confidence in the community pursuit of knowledge — and thus join the company of the builders of tomorrow.

As Julian Huxley understands:

" Progress has hitherto been a rare and fitful by-product of evolution. Man has the possibility of making it the main feature of his own future evolution, and of guiding its course in relation to a deliberate aim. . . .

" So far as our knowledge goes, human mind and personality are unique and constitute the highest product yet achieved by the cosmos. Let us not put off our responsibilities onto the shoulders of mythical gods or philosophical absolutes, but shoulder them in the hopefulness of tempered pride. . . . Our business in the world is seen to be the imposition of the best and most enduring of our human standards upon ourselves and our planet. The enjoyment of beauty and interest, the achievement of goodness and efficiency, the enhancement of life and its variety — these are the harvest which our human uniqueness should be called upon to yield."

As Peter the apostle put it, " Giving all diligence, add to your faith the virtue of knowledge." (II Peter 1:5, paraphrase.)

13

Fellowship Is the Goal and the Way
— Through Action

We are invited to fellowship (healing, satisfying, stimulating) with one God, one universe, one humanity, not only with our minds, but also with our muscles — not in words alone, but in deeds as well. Our deeds, so to speak, are motion pictures of what is going on in our minds. The thrust of the Holy Spirit in us creates and increases our fellowship, not in principle only, but in practice also. As James put it: " Be ye doers of the word, and not hearers only." (James 1:22, KJV.)

Fellowship through action is often "too little and too late," yet, when you stop to think about it, nothing worth achieving was ever achieved without it. We think of Jesus as a heroic individual "going it alone," yet twelve men walked and worked and finally suffered with him. He said to all of them, including Judas, "So far as I am concerned, you are not my servants, but my friends." (John 15:15, paraphrase.)

A creative person is usually the "starter" in every great enterprise, but he starts nothing unless others are willing to be started; as a matter of fact, it is by others that he himself was started. Even Jesus, for example, was not without a mother: Mary was the mother of his flesh, but two thousand years of Jewish history was the mother of his mind. The Old Testament was his only university; Abraham, Moses, David, and the prophets made him possible.

The past as well as the present always participates in our action, is always a member of our team. Hence, the past as well as the present is always entitled to be heard; very little is to be gained by listening to either alone. For this reason we have an Old as well as a New Testament. To achieve active teamwork between the past and the present is the central problem in education. Not often, but now and then, a student or a professor listens so carefully to a selected choir of voices speaking wisdom or folly out of the past that he fails to hold up his end of the conversation; he is simply Little Sir Echo; he contributes nothing of his own; the past is the ventriloquist and he is the dummy. A parrot can quote an authority; a well-trained parakeet can recite a creed; a human being, if he will, can think about it, talk back to it, sift it for its present value. More than once Jesus pointed out, " Moses told you one thing; I tell you another." He did not report or echo the Old Testament slavishly; rather he paid it the sincere compliment of treating it imaginatively, of thinking with it, in it, and about it. He changed neither jot nor tittle of its depth, but many a jot and tittle on its surface; in some real degree he altered both its letter and its law.

More commonly, a student (or a professor) is talking when he should be listening; he is so busy telling the world that it can never tell him what he needs to know; he is basically discourteous toward the past, refuses to allow it to speak freely, to hold up its end of the dialogue. As Jesus put it, " The man who is truly wise brings out of his treasure not only what is new but also what is old [Matt. 13:52, paraphrase]; he is interested in the latest, but even more in the truest word."

We are always fascinated by the intense drama of Jesus' life; Matt Dillon and Wyart Earp led longer, and more destructive, but not more active, lives. Thought was important to Jesus (frequently he spent all night thinking alone on a mountain), but action was not less important. And his action was never merely his own; Judaism also acted in him, with him, and against him. Historic Christianity, likewise, is not merely the action of Judaism and Jesus, but of the church as well — the community of reception and distortion. Whatever good has come into the world through Christianity has always been, and is now, a community product. That good, I think, is more easily underestimated than understood; it is also more easily rejected than reproduced.

Paul, at quick glance, appears a lonely fighter — to begin with *against* and later *for* the Christian fellowship. However, as the thirteenth apostle, the way was prepared for him by the first twelve. He reacted to them, and they to him. Two strands of Jewish influence molded his mind: the fundamentalism of the Pharisees, their readiness to persecute difference of opinion, but also the liberalism of Gamaliel, the will-to-love taught in the school of Hillel. There are no self-made men, though no one ever became creative without struggling to think truly, to act constructively.

The New Testament is marked by productive variety, not by sterile uniformity. Paul and Barnabas got along together about as well as diplomats at the councils of the United Nations. Paul and James did not see eye to eye. Paul and Peter were competitors as well as allies in the early church, and have retained their distinct character in Protestant and Roman Catholic Christendom. Human differences are sometimes important and often creative; they are always more exciting, and more constructive, than the dull indifference of dictatorship; their presence gives fellowship depth, breadth, height, movement, and local color — the breath of life. As many have failed to do, both in the first and in the twentieth centuries, Paul perceived that creative action is always a community enterprise, an affair of the Holy Spirit, the unity and energy of the Spirit in, and through, human diversity. He wrote:

" Now there are varieties of gifts, but the same Spirit; and there are varieties of service, but the same Lord; and there are varieties of working, but it is the same God who inspires them all in every one. To each is given the manifestation of the Spirit for the common good. To one is given through the Spirit the utterance of wisdom, and to another the utterance of knowledge according to the same Spirit, to another faith by the same Spirit, to another gifts of healing by the one Spirit, to another the working of miracles, to another prophecy. . . . All these are inspired by one and the same Spirit, who apportions to each one individually as he wills.

" For just as the body is one and has many members, and all the members of the body, though many, are one body, so it is with Christ. For by one Spirit we were all baptized into one body — Jews or Greeks, slaves or free — and all were made to drink of one Spirit." (I Cor. 12:4-13, RSV.)

Paul was even more specific. In his view, your body, my body, and the one body of mankind are made up of many parts, not of one only. The body itself is a team, and all its work is teamwork. " If the foot should say, ' Because I am not a hand, I do not belong to the body,' that would not make it any less a part of the body. And if the ear should say, ' Because I am not an eye, I do not belong to the body,' that would not make it any less a part of the body. If the whole body were an eye, where would be the hearing? If the whole body were an ear, where would be the sense of smell? . . . If all were a single organ, where would the body be? As it is, there are many parts, yet one body. The eye cannot say to the hand, ' I have no need of you,' nor again the head to the feet, ' I have no need of you.'. . . If one member suffers, all suffer together; if one member is honored, all rejoice together." (I Cor. 15-17, 19-21, 26, RSV.) For example, the fact that Russians, Chinese, and Africans are not Americans does not make them other than human. I have seen Americans rejoice at Russia's scientific achievement; why not? It is our human achievement. I have heard Russians lament America's scientific failure; why not? It is our human failure. Similarly, the fact that Hindus, Buddhists, and Moslems are not Methodists does not make them other than members of our human community. Their historic successes are our human successes; their tragic failures in India, China, and the Middle East are our human failures. As Paul knew, the whole of humanity is one family, one body. As Dostoevsky put it: " The people is the body of God."

The United States itself came into being through community action — across all kinds of diversity in greed and creed. The Civil War was produced by passionate difference of opinion; both North and South were powerful because they developed community action within their own spheres; when the hot war was over, and the cold war began, the recovery of political fellowship,

across shattering difference, made possible the ongoing of this nation — as one nation. Few people, I think, would really prefer
that we were forty-eight nations today — like Middle Africa,
Middle Europe, and the Middle East!

The United Nations came into existence, and will grow in effectiveness, through community action across wide economic and
cultural chasms. Every child has to crawl before it walks or runs.
The UN, after all, is only our second faltering attempt at factual
world brotherhood, our second effort to translate spiritual principle into political practice.

The Second World War was fought, and brought to an end,
by community action. Fellowship, it is obvious, is often the source
of sorrow; it sometimes strengthens inadequate loyalties and premature maturities; saints are seldom as thick as thieves; yet mankind has discovered, as yet, no other method of progress. The
short future need not but may mean tragedy; the long future can
mean only an increase of world community. As Reinhold Niebuhr has understood:

"Mankind will finally find political instruments and moral re-
sources adequate for a wholesome communal life on a world-wide
scale. But generations and centuries may be required to complete the
task. . . .

"The world community must be built by men and nations suffi-
ciently mature and robust to understand that political justice is
achieved, not merely by destroying, but also by deflecting, beguiling
and harnessing residual self-interest and by finding the greatest possible concurrence between self-interest and the general welfare. They
must also be humble enough to understand that the forces of self-
interest to be deflected are not always those of the opponent or competitor. They are frequently those of the self, individual or collective,
including the interests of the idealist who erroneously imagines himself above the battle."

Because common action is often mobilized in the pursuit of
lesser goals than world community and personal dignity, the creative repentance called honest self-criticism (the work of the Holy
Spirit) is a perpetual necessity, in whole societies as well as in individual souls. Too, we are taught by our failures as nations and

as men. Societies, to be sure, may be slower than individuals to evaluate their true worth and partial worthlessness, yet their problem is not different in kind. Self-evaluation, whether collective or individual, is usually both painful and productive. In the individual, a sensitive conscience (the mind's look at itself) plays the role of critic; nations are similarly confronted with conscience in the words and deeds of nonconformists. An individual often attempts to silence his inner critic; in the same way, society sometimes succeeds in silencing its nonconformists — though never for long. The truth will out; it is tougher than conformist crusades.

The honest self-criticism of nations often expresses itself in deeds as well as words. A nation resists change, but without it atrophies and decays. Americans today consider revolution, in any form, the one unpardonable sin. Every self-approving nation prefers what it calls " evolution " to what it calls " revolution." In Niebuhr's words, " Evolutionary millennialism is always the hope of [the] comfortable." The United States, however, was born in revolution — an open attack upon real or imagined tyranny. True, sporadic and bloody revolutions usually characterize people moved more by emotion than by reason, yet the right to advance evolution by means of revolution (when all other avenues are closed), is, according to the Declaration of Independence, God-given. Jefferson was quick to point out what, after all, is true — that men normally will long endure oppressive government rather than embark upon the perilous adventure of revolt; who can tell for certain what will happen on the other side of breakdown? Nonetheless, evil governments cannot bank forever on human acquiescence. Coercion, whether moral or military, can become a necessity when essential tyranny will not yield to persuasion. For this reason, Moses led a revolution against Pharaoh, the Christians against Caesar, Luther against papal absolutism, and Lenin against a corrupt Russian aristocracy.

For the same reason, the free world hopes for a revolt of Russian masses against the Kremlin, and secretly applauded (though failed to aid) the revolt of Hungary against foreign domination. Again in Niebuhr's words:

"It is probably not too severe a judgment to declare that no group within a nation will ever criticize the nation as severely as the nation ought to be criticized, if it does not stand partly outside of the nation. That is the strategic and moral significance of the proletarian class. . . .

"Equal justice is the most rational ultimate objective for society. If this conclusion is correct, a social conflict which aims at greater equality has a moral justification which must be denied to efforts which aim at the perpetuation of privilege. A war for the emancipation of a nation, a race, or a class is thus placed in a different category from the use of power for the perpetuation of imperial rule or class (or race) dominance."

The story of evolution is marked by sudden as well as slow change. Crisis is not unrelated to process; it is a stage within it. There is no uninterrupted progress, no continuity without breaks, in social history or in personal biography. In the Christian understanding of God, judgment is not unrelated to redemption; it is itself redemptive. "Solution" and "salvation" are two words with one meaning; no problem is solved until it is solved. And problems are sometimes solved suddenly as well as slowly. One can only conclude that *revolution is a stage in evolution* — one stage only, and to be avoided as long as possible, since it is usually more destructive than creative. The cost of revolution is great, but the cost of too-prolonged acquiescence in actual evil — whether collective or personal — is usually greater. From the beginning until now, in the face of totalitarianism, whether "democratic" or monarchial, whether "archaic" or "futuristic," as Peter and John put it, "We ought to obey God rather than men" (Acts 5:29, KJV).

The *qualitative* growth of world community, not mere *quantitative* extension, is and will remain the requirement of the Holy Spirit. We have thus far advanced, as a human race, not merely along straightaways, but also by the turning of sharp corners — even through long and painful detours.

Conversion itself (whether collective or individual) involves inevitable crisis, catharsis, and reconstruction; it is always both revolution and evolution at the same time — that is, it is preceded by preparation and followed by growth — as it was in Paul. You and I individually, and mankind as a whole, are now being converted — forward, toward ethical maturity, world community, the next stage in divine creation. Christianity itself is only secondarily creed and sacrament; it is primarily the Holy Spirit, God's "revolution forward," in our midst and in our minds — " the power of Love unto salvation" (Rom. 1:16, paraphrase) in co-operative civilizations and souls.

The goal is clear; clear also is the way. It is not an easy way; moral and material evolution is mountain-climbing, and mountain-climbing is breath-taking — as Dante, John Bunyan, and the conquerors of Mt. Everest understood. But to man at least, every other way is more difficult still; every other way turns out to be the broad way (the TV Tin Pan Alley) of moral ease and drift which leads only to destruction.

14

Fellowship Is the Goal and the Way
— in Devotion

That all men, and all nations, may learn to live responsibly, sympathetically, creatively, with one another — for what other cause came the Buddha, the prophets, and the Christ (with their churches) into the world? What other cause is great enough — than the brotherhood on earth of the maturing sons of God? A one-world political community can exist only on paper unless it is accompanied and reinforced by one-world spiritual community. As Jesus, in effect, described it, " My father's house *of many mansions* [the entire earth — and all the stars] shall be called the house of prayer *for all nations.*" (Mark 11:17, paraphrase.) Not only our churches of many faiths, but the earth itself " is the Lord's, and the fulness thereof; the world, and they that dwell therein "! The entire earth, our present and shrinking dwelling place, exists to become (much more than it is today) the house of fellowship — in devotion as in knowledge and action.

The churches of the Buddha, the prophets, and the Christ exist to lead the way to ethical world community — in the wisdom and strength of the Spirit. This is a big purpose, a big goal, but we are not always dealing with a small God. It is true, tragically true, that in our actual churches (of all faiths) small minds sometimes become smaller. Today, in the Middle East, for example, the children of Isaac and the children of Ishmael seem busily forgetting Abraham, their common ancestor. Religious difference seems to strengthen rather than weaken belligerence. It is true that in our churches the one world of Love, the responsible community that God is building, is sometimes shattered into a thousand frenzied fragments. Group egoism, or nationalism, is as understandable, even admirable, yet also as destructive, in totalitarian religions as in totalitarian states. It is true beyond belief that our churches are often busily engaged in secondary enterprises — the idolatry of mechanics, the substitution of means for ends. This is not at all surprising, for our religions, in large part, are our creations, bearing our image — as finite and fallible as we are! The truly surprising thing is not the humanity of our churches but their divinity; in some real degree they are also promoting the community and dignity of man in the hand, in the heart, of God!

Because men are in our churches (of all faiths), self-love, which divides and destroys, is more common than Love, which unites and heals. But our churches are not made up only of men. God also is in our churches, in every actual church. Because God is among us, *without end,* Love survives and leads and heals and quickens and enlarges in spite of defensive and destructive self-love. In all kinds of churches (Buddhist, Hindu, Moslem, Jewish, Catholic, Protestant, Unitarian, Ethical Culture Society, and Holy Roller) God is present and at work; he simply cannot be kept out — anywhere! He breaks through closed doors, and enters — to bless. And in every church he is both a stranger and at home. He is the uninvited guest — where men do not love their near and distant neighbors. He is the invited guest — where holy Love breaks through the tight compartments of human self-love, and creates one world.

Picture in your mind a chain with four links. The link nearest us is our present world of conflict, excessive acquisitiveness, and spiritual frustration — our century of standardized mediocrity. The fourth link (the link most distant from us) is our present world transfigured, made over, converted, completed by the divine achievement in man of dynamic, as against static, maturity — so far beyond our present experience that our finest prophets can only dimly see its broad outlines, the towers, so to speak, of the coming City of God. Between the link farthest away and the one near at hand are links three and four: necessarily *together,* these middle links are our organized churches (of all creeds) and our unorganized yet universal community of pioneers — out ahead of us, leading and pointing the way. They are God's men from tomorrow already among us, directing our traffic, through every political and cultural snarl, toward the earthly City of Light.

Each of the four links is the Church of God, at one stage or another of its development, for the thrust of creation, the Holy Spirit, is present everywhere, alike on the way and at the goal! Links two and three are therefore the visible and invisible church (the church of members known and counted, and the church of scientific and moral pioneers unknown and uncounted) — the church which began when men began, to begin anew with the prophets and the Christ, advance agents of spiritual world community.

The most important of the four links is the eventual one-world fellowship in justice and love, which God is building, and will complete, upon this earth. For this we pray when we say: " Thy will be done, on earth as it is in heaven." Next in importance is the link called the " fellowship of the seers " (scientific and spiritual) — within and beyond our churches — the informal society of those who lead the way to dignity and community. Third in importance (though none is dispensable) is the link representing our actual churches (of all faiths), our houses of prayer, our formal fellowships of memory and hope (that is, of creed and sacrament), where childhood faith is nurtured, distorted or corrected, and matured. Fourth in importance is the link nearest us — the whole round earth as it is, even now, with all its glory and vision, with all its ignorance and sin. For the earth, like the stars, is the Lord's, has always been, will always be. Not one of the links is unimportant, for each is the world God is building. In a very real sense, all the links are equally important, for childhood is of no less value than maturity!

No inevitable conflict exists between the church as creed, the church as magic ritual, cleansing from sin, providing peace of mind, and the church as the fellowship of those who, in some degree, hear and heed God's call to growing community. If creed has often prevented growth, creed itself can grow. If ritual has often looked backward *only,* better ritual also can look forward. If men have thought of God as wholly apart from the world, the discovery that God is the strength and moral vision of the world does not bring worship to an end; it puts worship to work; it harnesses the energy of devotion.

Our churches, then, form the middle term between the future and the present — between God's will for us and our will for ourselves, between one world struggling to be born and our resisting fragments, between final ethical community and each individual pilgrim today and every day.

Arnold J. Toynbee used the term "the Church" in precisely this sense when he described it as the Chrysalis between the dying Roman civilization and the European Christian civilization demanding to be born. The civilization of Greece and Rome had reached old age, and received the last rites of the Church on its deathbed. Within the womb of the Church a new civilization had been conceived, and in time was born. The Church was the middle term, the link, the living link, between the Rome of the Caesars and the Rome of the Christians.

The full church (you might call it the "link of first importance") does not yet exist upon this earth. God *is now creating it.* History not only passes over into theology, but is itself theological; further, it is history, the human enterprise, which is now on its way, in God's keeping, through and beyond its endless deviations, its partial destructions, to the threshold of promised fulfillment. It is history, the human pilgrimage, which is now being transmuted from base metal into gold. The full church on its way to us will be history itself gaining and receiving completion. As Revelation describes it: " I, John, saw the holy city, new Jerusalem, coming down from God out of heaven, prepared as a bride adorned for her husband. And I heard a great voice out of heaven saying, Behold, the dwelling place of God is in, and with, all men *on earth,* and he shall dwell not above them nor apart from them but among them and in them, and they shall be his people brought to human maturity, and God himself (not another) shall be with them all, and be their God. . . . And he that sat upon the throne said, Behold, I make *all things new*. . . . My offspring, humanity, shall overcome, and inherit, all things; I will be his God, and he shall be my son." (Rev. 21:2, 3, 5, 7, KJV, paraphrase.)

When you are looking at recurrent threats outside us and within, it is all but impossible to believe that God has not started an enterprise too big for him to finish. The short view scares us. When you are looking at God the Universe, the Father Almighty, you know that not to believe is blasphemy. If the single incarnation was both possible and inevitable, the eventual total incarnation (which all religions promise, for which all pray) is both possible and inevitable as well. As Lecomte du Noüy and Albert Schweitzer have understood, " Sooner or later there must dawn the true and final Renaissance which will bring peace to the world."

Through all our fragments God *is now creating* one church, one fellowship, one brotherhood including all religions, all races, all philosophies, all sciences, all governments — a universal fellowship of love, a classless society, the image of God. For God, it appears, seeks not the cancellation of our differences, but their fulfillment in community. The Garden of Eden is ahead of us, not behind us: God is now creating it. And he has the power to finish what he has thus far so nobly advanced — not in escape from our freedom, but through our freedom; not without tragedy, but through and beyond tragedy.

You and I, often enough, worship our fragment, our part, and deny the whole enterprise of God. God wills the universal church not yet fully created, and God is sufficient to complete it — not in escape from history, but through history. The full church is not yet here, but it is on the way; there are streaks of dawn shining in our predawn — our Dark Ages. God's full truth is ahead of us. " I believe in the holy catholic church," means exactly this: the universal church is now being created through and beyond our confusion; the universal church must inevitably appear, for God *is* God!

The church (the link of second importance) is the fellowship of men and women, in all lands, races, and religions, in whom and through whom the Holy Spirit offers healing to humanity. Through the saints, now underproduced in our midst, God, *Agapē,* the Holy Spirit, moves quietly among us, creating out of our chaos the universal church. "The communion of saints," means exactly this. Through the community of saints (known only to God) *Agapē* embraces the fragments of the present and creates the church of the future. The pioneers are both within our churches, and beyond them. To the saints, there is little difference between our churches and our secular cultures: God owns both, and both are incomplete. To the saint, there is no difference between what is called sacred and what is called secular; both are sacred; both are areas of divine action, theaters of divine operation.

People who think of themselves as holy are more secular than they realize; people who think of themselves as secular are more holy than they know. No white line between saint and sinner exists for the saint; he knows himself to be an imperfect servant among saints and sinners alike — and to both equally. To the saint, there is only one world, and all of it is God's — God's educational institution, God's school, where men and civilizations prepare in theory and practice for membership in the eventual church universal.

The church (the link of third importance) is the world of our churches, our fragments of the future, whether Greek, Russian, Roman, Lutheran, Calvinist, or Anglican (whether Hindu, Buddhist, Moslem, or Jew). Whatever the label on the bottle, the bottle may be empty! In our churches, the incompleteness of creation is self-evident. Our churches, at present, are incomplete in knowledge, in ethics, in charity, in usefulness — in anything and everything. We churchmen do not possess God; he possesses us, and tolerates our stupidities and sins while he educates us and the world, while he creates in the present his church of the future.

In our churches, the past and the future meet — and often in head-on collision!

The church (the link of fourth importance) is the entire universe — as we now know it. The total universe, as it is, belongs utterly to God, is the omnipresence of God. He is the life in all that lives, the power to exist in all that exists. The universe is a great cathedral — a cosmic prayer. This planet is our chapel within the cathedral. Every man, by birth, is a member of the family of God, within his care and control; every man is on the way; every man is enrolled in God's grammar school; every man is learning; every man is growing toward or away from God; every man is of the past or of the future; every man dwells all the days of his life in the hollow of God's hand.

Our churches sometimes regard themselves as *tests* of faith. Often enough, and embarrassingly enough, our actual creeds seem to be " cosmic foot rules " by which we define ourselves as " the elect " and the rest of humanity as " the damned." But what do you expect of adolescents? If we were already all that we are to become, there would be no need for our churches in the first place. We live in the age of the missing link, the age of man, the mammal who has read a book; it is therefore almost impossibly difficult for us to acknowledge in public that our creeds are not final tests, but more or less *fervent testimonies* of true faith. To be halfway to sanity, halfway to maturity, is better than not to have started. It is God who is calling us to growth. It is he who sustains us in the present, as he has in the past. The human enterprise is his undertaking. He brought forth the mammal out of the amoeba. It is therefore not irrational but wholly rational to hold the conviction that he will bring forth, in time, the ethical world community out of our present divisive and destructive fragments. He can be trusted. He will finish what he has begun. Nothing can prevent the completion of his creation. His future for us breaks through, deepens us, widens our horizons, enriches us, makes us more human, in spite of all our resistance, and all this he does for us in the midst of the struggle of the world — in our actual churches, and in the fellowship of the saints, the seers, the pioneers, the holy ones he has sent us from the future.

All these actual churches (of all faiths), with all their follies and foibles, yet also with their heroes and saints and pioneers, are (as John Wesley described them) not ends, but " means of grace "; they bridge the chasm between God's final one world, the community of the sons of God, and our individual and lonely little souls. Our churches, even now, end our individual isolation from the final community, restore our dignity, our status as men. Even now, they make us not merely products, not merely problems, but also participants in the enterprise of creation.

We live in an age of increasing collectivism — the age of science and society. Personhood, as such, seems a dead issue, a lost cause. Indeed, you will not find it a simple matter to maintain your personal integrity, the recognition of yourself as an ultimate value to God and man, the recognition, in some sense, of your individual indispensability! Our churches of all faiths keep faith, including faith in self, alive! In our churches we *ascend* to meet — and are often taller together than apart.

Outside our churches (our communities of devotion) the world seems, and assumes that it is, secular, scientific, and flat. If I live only in that world, I no longer exist as a man, a thinking human being, a son of God, a child of the future. Neither science, as such, nor society, as such, seems to give a tinker's curse whether I live or die. Within our churches, the world seems, and is, more than secular, more than scientific, more than flat. Within a church, my soul can breathe: I am more than a vote, more than a consumer, a statistic, a ticket, a mechanic. Within a church, I am a man, a member of God's family. My existence is recognized as of great potential value; my personhood is regarded as an end, not a means, as in some sense indispensable. Within a church, my selfhood is not crushed by science and society but restored by the breath of God. Within a church, God breathes into my nostrils, as he did at the dawn of creation, and I become a *living* soul.

Without a church, I am in part isolated, as a self, from the future ethical community; without a church, the future community is in part isolated from me. A church ends my isolation from mankind, and the isolation of mankind from me. A church preserves my life, though I die, for the church universal is the immortality of mankind; it has within it, in the " communion of saints," every member who has ever lived, every member who now lives, and every member who will ever live; as the guide and guardian of the growing person, it represents every member of the human race — past, present, and future, for not church members only but all men are called to growth in love. Outside a church, the soul sometimes dies before the body (and this is called " the second death "). Within a church, the body comes alive in the soul, for the future does not begin in the future; it begins now.

Our churches bear the same relation to the coming world community that primitive societies bore for half a million years to the first beginnings of civilization. Precisely this relation our churches enable us, individually, to share.

The past is not dead, as Matthew Arnold believed; it is very much alive in our bodies, our minds, and our institutions. The future and I meet in a church. There, at prayer and Holy Communion, I no longer merely exist; I live, breathe, walk, and work with God and with the man he is creating and will complete in his image.

The *thrust* of divine creation, present everywhere, is intensified where men gather to pray, to worship, to hear and heed God's word, to seek their full stature as his sons, to let the light of the future, of ethical world community, play upon their hearts, wash away their defensive self-love, create in them an unconquerable resolve to lift rather than drift. Within and beyond your local church, you have felt this *thrust* since childhood; when and where you felt it, whether weakly or vividly, the Spirit of the living God was moving within you.

Conclusion

15

The Holy Thrust to Freedom and Fellowship

Everyone wants to be up to date — in dress, for example, if not in ideas. A few men are concerned to be as up to date as possible — in religion. Not outwardly or superficially, for fashions change (in church architecture, for instance), but inwardly, deeply, permanently. By what standard, then, shall each of us determine whether his personal religion is mildewed and moth-eaten or really up to date?

The measure of an up-to-date Christian is not the arrogance with which he denounces other faiths; it is not the orthodoxy of his creed ("the devils also believe," said James); it is not even the orthopraxy (the correctness) of his conduct; it is not the energy he puts into good works; it is not the emotion he releases in hymn-singing. The true standard, the exact test, was given by Paul: "If any man have not the Spirit of Christ [*Now!*], he is none of his" (Rom. 8:9, KJV).

There are two kinds of Christians: one looks backward, with grateful memory enshrined in sacrament and dogma; the other has no interest in the "pastness" of the past, but looks and moves *forward,* is *now* possessed by the Spirit of Christ, by explosive faith and hope and love with *impact* in the modern world! A Christ who does not challenge or rule the minds of men today has no reality — is a long time dead! Unless Christ *now* makes altruists out of egoists, *now* creates Schweitzers and Father Damians out of garden-variety humans, all the churches, all the clergy, all the folk who mouth dogmas and mime rituals add up to nothing, and less than nothing.

The Spirit of Christ is and produces a perpetual moral revolution in mind and life and social structure. Where moral revolution is dead, Christ is dead also, and the churches which preserve his memory neither have life nor are capable of giving life. Christ lives only where moral revolution is now taking place — in all kinds of institutions, both secular and sacred, and in all kinds of men, both sinners and saints. The explosive presence and power of continued and increasing revolution — *forward* toward breadth of brotherhood and depth of freedom — this, and only this, is faith, hope, and love worth having; this, and only this, is true religion, true science, and true government.

The *thrust forward* — toward the unachieved will of God on earth — this alone is the Holy Spirit; it exists only where it moves actual groups and actual men — from within. Wherever it exists, it is moral dynamite; it explodes; it changes the face of the world; it alters the imaginations of men. The name of this dynamite is Love — not the effeminate sentiment, not the soft emotion, rather the will of steel, the "intestinal fortitude," the sanctified stubbornness to be satisfied with nothing less than ethical world community and personal self-respect. Men who are content with mediocrity and conformity — with things as they are, and themselves as they are — know nothing of the Spirit, no matter how often they repeat the Apostles' Creed in private or in public. The *thrust forward* toward the practical growth of love, outwardly and inwardly — this specifically is the Spirit of Christ, bequeathed to nations and men open to receive it, to move with it, and be moved by it. Jesus' first disciples were scarcely prepared to receive the Spirit, hardly recognized it when it came, attempted to imprison it within Judaism (Acts 10:45; 11:8, 9, 17, 18; 15:1 f.) — yet were changed by it, in spite of themselves, from isolated fishermen to the forerunners of one world. More of the future than of the present was in Jesus' mind when he breathed upon his disciples, and said: "Receive ye the Holy Ghost" (John 20:22, KJV).

The *thrust toward fellowship* with each man and all men, in every land, language, and religion — this Spirit unites men separated by nationalism and dogmatism, replaces anarchy with community, lifts serfs and slaves to equality with their masters. " A humble man has no inferiors." A college student wrote these words in an assigned essay; I have not read truer words in any religious classic. " A humble man has no inferiors " — since all are equal before God; the thrust toward fellowship makes democrats of all aristocrats; and vice versa — since a humble man also has no superiors. Serfs, wage slaves, and exploited folk of every race and nation stand upon their feet, look out upon their fellow men from a position of equal dignity, dedicated to equal justice.

The forward thrust, the Spirit of Christ, evokes true self-love against every form of " Uriah Heep " or pseudo humility; it raised the Roman proletariat to equal status with their rulers and brought tyranny to an end. Christianity did indeed destroy the Roman Empire, as Gibbon knew, though not for the " pacifist " reason he imagined. The strait jacket of the Roman social structure — with its system of masters and slaves — burst at the seams before the onslaught of moral revolution, the discovery of selfhood and self-respect among the Christian poor. Simple claustrophobia (fear of suffocation), engendered by Christian selfhood, shattered the Roman caste system. It was war to the death; either the moral revolution or the Roman Empire had to yield; the revolution proved the tougher; Rome cracked and fell in pieces. In our time, also, every empire that resists world community and personal dignity must, and will, similarly yield.

The Christian thrust, more revolutionary than communism, will open the closed corporation of Russian dictatorship and release again the breath of personal freedom; it will thus turn lock step collectivism into the possibility of community. The Christian thrust will open also the closed self-righteousness of capitalist mammon worship, end the solitary mental confinement of conformist oaths and loyalty crusades, and release personal freedom in productive community. American Christian claustrophobia will destroy the " protective custody " called " thought control."

Jesus knew that men would worship him as a substitute for doing his will, an easy alternative to thinking and acting with him, a pious escape from the thrust of moral revolution — *the only Holy Spirit in God or man.* He might have said, " Not every one that saith unto me, Lord, Lord, shall enter the fellowship of the forward thrust." (Matt. 7:21, KJV, paraphrase.)

Jesus specifically defined the Spirit, the Holy Spirit, that would fall upon his disciples in all ages, take possession of them, and set them ablaze with revolutionary zeal. He said: " The words that I speak unto you, they are spirit, and they are life." (John 6:63, KJV.) Naturally, his disciples ignored, or failed to hear, what he said; often enough, students in every age have ignored, or failed to hear, their teacher's words. College professors call this " the breakdown of communication." What is spoken and what is heard bear little resemblance. " The words that I speak," said Jesus, *the words themselves,* " are spirit and life." For words are ideas, and ideas have legs. Ideas have consequences. Deeds proceed from words, and the words of life are life-giving. Jesus' words ignited in the hearts of men the flame of freedom which Rome's fire brigades were unable to put out. The real fire of Rome was not the one Nero started to destroy a city out-of-date; the real fire of Rome was the one Christ started in Roman minds, the fire of Love which melted an iron caste system and brought selfhood and self-respect to birth and growth.

Death is not so important as life is, and the strength — for good or ill — that flows from it. Jesus died, but strength has continued to flow from his life; his death only increased the *forward thrust* of his words, of his Spirit, in the institutions and imaginations of earthly men.

It is no cause for wonder that Buddhists feel the same way about Buddha. He too was claimed by death, yet strength has continued to flow from him, and increase in the words and deeds of his disciples. To them, time has shown that his spirit, too, is a moral revolution moving explosively in soul and society. Buddha lives — to develop men morally big in a civilization morally worthy of them. Where does Buddha live? They answer, Where his words take possession of hearts and wills, and *today* widen and deepen men's ethical foundations. No matter how often the devout repeat Buddha's name in song and story, in pilgrimage and holy ritual, Buddha is dead, unless his words release the revolution *forward* in human life.

Moses was, and is, the spiritual father (or grandfather) of three great peoples — the Jews, the Christians, and the Moslems. As Freud understood, Moses' ethical universalism, the Ten Commandments, countered and partially annulled by Jewish tribalism, renewed itself in Christ, the Moses after Moses. The words of the Prophet Mohammed, the Arabs' second Moses, form the moral revolution, the holy thrust, the Holy Spirit, in Islamic minds. The spirit of Moses, the words of Moses, *now* move and rule more than superficially in Europe, Africa, and the Americas. More men today believe in the Ten Commandments than in the Christ who fulfilled them and taught us that love is their fulfillment.

We can never understand communists until we realize that, in their view, the words of the prophet Karl Marx, renewed in Lenin, form the revolutionary thrust in Russia and China — the spirit which is holy to them — whether creative or destructive in itself. In the eyes of devout communists, Karl Marx was another Moses after Moses, for his central word was Moses' word: " Thou shalt not steal " (Ex. 20:15, KJV).

The spirit of moral revolution, the holy thrust of the life-giving Word, is often countered by feats of mental or social engineering. A chief characteristic of the Holy Spirit, however, is its power to break through every barricade erected to resist it. Thus the Christian revolution, with its insistence on personal freedom and universal fellowship, burst through the tomb of the Roman police state; will it not similarly burst through the tomb of the Russian police state — and through every religious or political structure, in East or West, built to withstand it?

In two ways, the Spirit of any people, the Spirit that *moves* in any man, can be identified: if it overcomes every individual and collective effort to resist it, if it increases the moral stature of individual men, and creates wider community — it is the Spirit of

God; if it decreases individual stature, and resists or delays one family of man, it is the spirit of evil.

We humans have come a long way in time, but a short way in the ability to get along with one another, and the ability to get along with ourselves. One power thrusts us *forward,* as groups and individuals, toward deeper freedom and wider fellowship, and cannot be stopped; one power will make our partly painful planet a better province in paradise: that one power is the moral revolution, the Holy Spirit, the holy mind, the holy word of the Savior and the saints — the word of Love, released in " secular " as well as " sacred " movements and men. As Jesus put it: " You shall receive power [the power to *progress,* the power to improve, the power to move and keep moving, the power to *grow* as nations, as churches, and as persons] when the Holy Spirit has come upon you; and you shall be my witnesses . . . to the end of the earth, and to the end of time." (Acts 1:8, RSV, paraphrase.)

REFERENCES

References

In this volume reference is made to the following sources, listed in the order of their use.

Chapter 3
> Dorothy L. Sayers, *Creed or Chaos?*, p. 15. Harcourt, Brace and Company, Inc., 1949.

Chapter 4
> Sigmund Freud, *A General Introduction to Psychoanalysis*, p. 320. Boni & Liveright, 1924.
> Roland H. Bainton, *Here I Stand*, p. 103, and *passim*. Abingdon Press, 1950.
> Richard Crossman, editor, *The God That Failed*, pp. 13–164. Harper & Brothers, 1950.

Chapter 5
> Alan Barth, *The Loyalty of Free Men*, p. 248. Viking Press, 1951.
> Arnold Toynbee, *A Study of History*, Vol. III, p. 201; Vol. IV, p. 301. Oxford University Press, 1939.

Chapter 6
> C. S. Lewis, *The Great Divorce*, p. 83. The Macmillan Company, 1946.
> Nels F. S. Ferré, *The Christian Understanding of God*, p. 222. Harper & Brothers, 1951.
> Pitirim A. Sorokin, *The Crisis of Our Age*, p. 27. E. P. Dutton & Co., Inc., 1951.

François Fénelon, *Christian Perfection,* p. 14. Harper &
Brothers, 1947.

C. S. Lewis, *Christian Behavior,* p. 69. The Macmillan Company, 1943.

Chapter 7

Roland H. Bainton, *op. cit.,* p. 144.

G. K. Chesterton, *Orthodoxy,* p. 151. Dodd, Mead & Company, Inc., 1927.

T. S. Eliot, *The Idea of a Christian Society,* p. 22. Harcourt,
Brace and Company, Inc., 1940.

Katherine Lee Bates, " O Beautiful for Spacious Skies."

Chapter 11

Fyodor Dostoevsky, *The Brothers Karamazov,* tr. by Con-
stance Garnett, p. 74. Modern Library, Inc., 1943.

Thomas Hobbes, *An Historical Narration Concerning Heresy,* p. 387. Academic Reprints, 1954.

Reinhold Niebuhr, *The Nature and Destiny of Man,* II,
p. 122. Charles Scribner's Sons, 1951.

Hendrik Kraemer, *Religion and the Christian Faith,* pp. 72–
96 and *passim.* The Westminster Press. 1956.

Chapter 12

Julian Huxley, *Man in the Modern World,* p. 28. Harper &
Brothers, 1955.

Chapter 13

Reinhold Niebuhr, *The Signs of the Times,* p. 56. Charles
Scribner's Sons, 1946.

Reinhold Niebuhr, *The Children of Light and the Children
of Darkness,* p. 186. Charles Scribner's Sons, 1944.

Reinhold Niebuhr, *Moral Man and Immoral Society,* p. 62.
Charles Scribner's Sons, 1936.

Chapter 14

Albert Schweitzer, *Out of My Life and Thought,* tr. by
C. T. Campion, p. 185. Henry Holt & Co., Inc., 1933.